PSYCHOLOGICALLY INFORMED ENVIRONMENTS FROM THE GROUND UP

ROBIN JOHNSON

PSYCHOLOGICALLY INFORMED ENVIRONMENTS FROM THE GROUND UP

SERVICE DESIGN FOR COMPLEX NEEDS

Fertile Imagination Press

Copyright © 2023 by Robin Johnson

All rights reserved. No part of this book may be reproduced in any manner whatsoever without written permission except in the case of brief quotations embodied in critical articles and reviews.

First Printing, 2023

CONTENTS

one — Preface
1

two — Introduction
4

three — Ideas in practice
8

four — What is the PIElink?
20

five — Five core themes
38

six — Introducing the PIEs approach
62

seven — Good questions
70

eight — Pizazz and the PIE Abacus
88

nine — The future for PIEs
107

CONTENTS

ten — Postscript
112

About The Author
114

CHAPTER ONE

PREFACE

This book is intended as an introduction to the world of 'psychologically informed environments' - 'PIEs' - not just a new name, but a whole new way of thinking about the work of services for people with complex needs.

But PIEs come in all shapes and sizes, many and varied; and this can cause some confusion when people come new to the idea. Even more so when they find they are now expected to 'be' one, but with little indication of what that is supposed to mean, in practice, in any given context or service.

This book therefore aims to dispel some of that confusion, firstly by going to the heart and spirit of the creative work being done already by many services in meeting sometimes very complex psychological and emotional needs.

Then we get on to explore the more detailed framework of ideas that we have developed in trying to capture, spread and encourage that constructive engagement; and some of the tools, such as the Pizazz - the PIEs services audit and development process - and the software version, the PIE Abacus, to help audit and develop services.

I was the original author of the term PIE, back in 2010; and I have been the 'chief steward' of how it has evolved since the first suggestion that this phrase offered a new way to see what was happening. But you'll note that in writing this, for the main body of the book, I will instead use the word 'we'.

This is because the ideas I have been outlining have come from hundreds, possibly thousands of conversations over the past ten, twenty or more years. I believe these are not my ideas, but yours; I have simply been the one who tried to put them into words. People do say that I 'invented' or 'created' PIE; but as I see it, that's not really true. You all did. I was just the one to give it a name.

It's true that developing the PIEs frameworks - plural, because there are actually two that we tend to use, as I will explain - was largely my work. But in the end, they are both just descriptions of the work of others, and they arose out of those hundreds of conversations. Though the conclusions were mine, the work being described was not.

Recently we have been hearing that using the Pizazz can be a very effective way to help staff get to grips with what the PIE approach and framework can mean in practice, for any one particular service or network. But even the Pizazz was not all my own work. It was a blending of the PIEs approach with an existing software 'platform' for service-led service development - the iAbacus -that had its roots in education.

Again, I can take credit only for spotting it, and seeing the potential; though then it took some three years and more of adaptation, development, testing etc. to arrive at the software version, the PIE Abacus, which for me is one of the most exciting developments of all. More on that later, as they say.

My subject here, PIEs, is so multi-facetted, and the issues so inter-woven, that in places this account may seem repetitive, with the same connection being made in many places, from different angles. If this becomes tedious, even irksome, I can only apologise; but the inter-connectedness of everything is the subject, after all.

A book, like a conversation, is an environment for ideas. But in a live conversation the participants can constantly shift the focus and the language to gauge, respond, reach out and engage the others. In a book we cannot do this, and we must just try our best to pitch it at a level that we may hope may engage as many as possible.

I know I can't get it just right for everyone, every time; and I'm sure I haven't. That's why I stress here constantly that it's quite OK to dip in and out of this book, come back to some bits only when you are ready to go a little further.

In the end, as I say somewhere here: these words are our servants, not our masters; and there is really only one fundamental 'PIE principle', which is to think for yourself about what you can do with the ideas here. In the end, as in the beginning, this is your work.

Robin Johnson

August 2023,
Falmouth, Cornwall

CHAPTER TWO

INTRODUCTION

This book aims to provide an introduction to the ideas and the practice of a 'psychologically informed environment' - a PIE - for those quite new to the very idea. Here we hope to set you on course for understanding the basics of what we mean by a PIE, and what it might mean for you, and your service or services.

That said, even those already fairly familiar with the basics may well find in these pages that the description here, with the most up-to-date summaries of where we are at, may still hold something new for you, to stimulate and to encourage further exploration.

The other principal intentions here are to introduce the PIElink, the community of practice website 'for all things PIE', and the Pizazz, the team-based design process that we have created for service-led appraisal, review and development.

In Chapter Three there is some general background for those thinking to take your first steps in this direction, beginning with the underlying spirit of the thing. There is also a little on the history, and the on-going development of these ideas, to put this all in context – and hence the title of this chapter: 'Ideas in practice'.

Chapter Four then provides an introduction to the PIElink itself. This is a uniquely valuable resource to know and explore - and it is still the only website in the world entirely devoted to informing and supporting a constantly growing, constantly evolving community of practice in the development of PIEs.

With chapter titles in this book matching pages on the site, we can show you where you can pick up and follow any thread there, to pursue your own interests. These links are simply too numerous to include here in the book, as constant references to these items and their locations would rapidly clog up the pages. But on the website you can rummage around freely for whatever you might find useful.

There are several dozen practice examples given here, just an indication of the wide range of activities and innovations in practice that we have found particularly telling. Here, for the book, we have selected a few - but more to whet your appetite than to satisfy it. On the PIElink pages and in the members' library we have many more illustrations of elements of the PIEs approach in practice - including video, which we obviously cannot include in a book.

Then in Chapter Five you will find the core themes of the PIE framework spelled out in some detail. These are the issues that we find it's most helpful to address. In Chapters Six and Seven we will go a little further, to look at some of the issues and questions that arise for those tasked with introducing the

PIE approach in any service or agency. The questions here may also be helpful for anyone who is interested in the wider context and ideas behind it all.

In Chapter Eight, there's an introduction to the Pizazz process. This is one of the key tools we have now developed for self-assessment, audit and development of services as PIEs. We begin with outlining the pen-and-paper version - which is free to download, from the website - and then explore the potential in the software version of the Pizazz, the PIE Abacus, taking us beyond assessment of single services to sharing the learning on what works, and what is needed.

If all that may sound a little intimidating, perhaps a bit too advanced for beginners, the emphasis here is firmly on *self*-assessment, and on service-led development. In fact, many services find that the easiest way to understand what the PIE approach can mean for them is to start by applying it via a Pizazz assessment.

Chapter Nine then looks towards the future. There is a continuous evolution, with the ideas and practice of PIE now growing into new areas, and here we look at the role of the PIElink itself, as the home of a community of practice. In the digital age, when live streaming of lively discussions makes possible developments and dialogues with action learning at the core, the future is open.

But we can take the suggestion of using the website a step further. The recent re-design and website links here allow us to future proof the content of this book, by indicating links to the areas of the site where new issues and new material will appear. It is here that the linkage between the website and this book becomes most useful.

It may be natural to aim to read this book through from beginning to end. But it's equally fine to just thumb through, to find what most interests you - just as, on the website itself, you can freely browse around the whole thing. The difference is that on the website you will find many more links, with more detail, discussion points, questions and threads.

But the important thing is to go at your own pace, take your own time in exploring all the material here; and for now, take from it only what you find useful.

When you are ready to go further, it's all there.

IDEAS IN PRACTICE

What exactly is a PIE?

But first, let's ask the obvious question: what exactly IS a PIE anyway?

The answer is simple, but rather unhelpful: being a PIE is not an exact thing. What it means will vary according to where you are, how you work, and who you work with. It's like pouring water into a cup - the water takes the shape of the cup.

This is why here we will start with the broad picture, the spirit of the thing, and something of the history - why and how these ideas and these services have developed in recent years. Then we will go on to give some examples; and then outline the overall framework that has now developed, to help you in looking at your own service (or services) in this new light.

All social environments

We do tend to say - this quote is taken from the website, the PIElink - that at its heart a psychologically informed environment is 'one that takes into account the psychological make-up - the thinking, emotions, personalities and past experience - of its participants, in the way it operates.'

But all human social environments do that to some degree. The human brain is wired to be exceptionally sensitive to the social world, and by far the most significant environment for human beings is other human beings. This is why we now tend to reserve the phrase for those environments - those places and services - that do so consciously, and that aim to develop their services 'in the round', in the ways we identify here.

Nevertheless it is worth bearing in mind from the outset that a lot of this is quite normal, completely natural to us as humans. Empathy is not a specialism. One thing we do want to stress from the start is how much of what we describe here as a PIE was already happening, long before we coined the term PIE to describe it. Much of it still is, without realising it's 'PIE'd'.

The aim of the PIEs idea, and then the detailed framework that has developed over the past 10+ years, was simply to help us focus more on what seems to work best. Later in this book we will look over some of the ways we have set out to help services do that; but for now, the point is that many find that much of this is 'stuff we already knew - we just didn't know we knew'.

PIEs in progress

Still, what this will mean for an outline of PIEs is that you can approach the PIEs phenomenon from several different angles; or at different levels of analysis, like the various layers of a map.

At one level, we have the many, many services that are actually operating with one or more of the elements of this way of working that we attempt to describe here: and usually with more than one. As we will see, these various aspects of the work do tend to go together - to form a whole.

But not all of them will actually call themselves PIEs. Many, outside the UK, may never even have heard the phrase; but they have learned what works for them. Now, though, there are increasingly many agencies that are consciously using the ideas in this approach to help think through how they are working - whatever their particular work may be.

This may also be happening at almost any level within the chain of command, from workers at the 'frontline', looking to share their thoughts and learn from other and/or to flag up concerns, through to middle and senior managers, and to funders looking to see how to encourage flexible and responsive services. One thing we have learned to appreciate is the value of the PIE approach being 'embedded' throughout all tiers and even all departments in a large agency.

In a number of areas we are now finding local networks of different services looking at using this way of thinking to share their concerns, and then seek ways to work better together. The PIEs idea, the spirit and the framework, then help to provide a shared language that can help different services find their common ground.

Some people talk here of 'working with' or even of 'implementing' the 'PIE principles' But as you will see, we tend to say there is really only one PIE principle: that you must think and decide for yourselves what you might do. All the rest of the ideas here are just the tools that you can use. The ideas that we have developed in more detail are not handed down in tablets of stone; they are just handy aids to thinking about the services we have.

The tools for the job

Foremost in that toolbox is the collection of observations of what works that we call the PIEs framework. This is the best account we have currently of all the things that, when taken together, make for a PIE.

You might think of these concepts as a lens through which to look at your own services. But a lens is not a checklist of things you must do to be a PIE. Like a pair of glasses, you just use them to look through.

In fact there has been a gradual evolution of these ideas, in a constant dialogue with the services that use them. This is why for the current framework we use a phrase borrowed from software development; we call it 'PIEs 2.0'.

As we'll see, this framework suggests five core 'themes', and fifteen or so key aspects (or 'practice elements') of a service and its work, as the things you might want to consider; and these are grouped under those five themes. It's not always a very neat fit - life is not neat, and complex needs tend to generate complex responses - but it generally seems to work; and it certainly covers a lot of ground.

To understand better this range and variety it may help at this stage to have at least a little of the history, and the evolution over time of the core of ideas.

An evolving picture

In the last decade or so of the 20th century in the UK, a number of different strands in our understanding of mental health began to come together. One was a growing recognition of the extent of poor mental health in the general population, but with particular concentrations in some quarters.

The exciting promise of community care, replacing the dilapidated and discredited institutionalised psychiatric hospital legacy of the previous century, was faltering through lack of funds, and what new services there were found themselves only able to focus on the most severe and most clearly defined mental illnesses.

Despite or even perhaps because of this, there was a slowly growing acknowledgement of the extent to which ordinary ('frontline') staff in a range of human services were dealing day-to-day with many of these more complex and un-met needs. Some, in fact, seemed to be rising to the challenge; and even getting quite good at it; and we found this, for example, in some homelessness services.

At the same time, there was a growing understanding of the nature of psychological and emotional trauma, making visible the long shadow that early and prolonged abuse and neglect may cast over the experience and the life chances of individuals subject to traumatising experiences in childhood.

An action learning approach

The key point to make here is that some services outside the mental health services did seem to be learning valuable lessons in how to work with these more complex needs, in developing approaches that the mainstream mental health services, focussed instead on other needs, had not been doing.

But at that time there was no really clear way to describe this. There was no common vocabulary of 'what works', and any descriptions that there were might be scattered across a patchwork of 'best practice' promptings and guidelines in different sectors, usually relevant only to that particular sector and the specific jurisdiction of the authorities, the funding or regulatory bodies in each sphere.

In one area, however, there was very rapid progress; this was in homelessness services. This was an area where the least attempt had been made until then to identify positive, let alone exciting or even cutting edge community mental health work. Despite this - or perhaps even because of this - the lessons being learned were fresher, and relatively free of the inertia of past thinking.

In 2010 the UK government issued a guidance document for homelessness services, aiming to recognise the extent of un-met need and 'complex trauma' in this population. With its lengthy (and distinctly unexciting) title: 'Non-statutory guidance on meeting the psychological and emotional needs of people who are homeless', this document was an attempt to identify and to promote what the authors saw of an emerging new way of working. To describe what we were seeing in some homelessness services, and hoped to encourage, this guidance document then adopted a phrase taken from a recent paper being published in a mental health journal.

To indicate to the intended readership - more conventional or mainstream mental health services - what the authors saw as happening outside the range of mental health care, this journal paper had coined the phrase a 'psychologically informed environment'; and we gave the developments in homelessness services as the example.

Is it still mainly about homelessness?

You will find that much of the content on the PIElink website describes how we have developed services in the UK to meet the challenge of homelessness. This was the sector where the PIE approach was first identified and named, and where it has had most immediate impact. It's here that the PIEs practice framework was first fully developed, and the first accounts, that we now call 'PIEs One', did focus largely on work in this area.

But although it was in this sector that we first started to identify the key issues, what we see here is not just about homelessness. The underlying ideas and practice that gave rise to the term PIE are actually far more widespread; and PIEs in other fields are equally valuable. Whatever context you may be working in, on the PIElink's pages you should find plenty of advice, examples, inspiration, some training materials and other 'food for thought', to help you on your way.

Certainly the PIE approach does seem particularly useful for services that work with people with quite complex emotional and psychological needs; and the PIE approach gave recognition to the work being done in homelessness in addressing these needs. But all human needs are complex. In the end, it's not about the needs, it's about the humanity.

As these ideas were being formulated over a couple of years, that description in itself seemed to spur on many services to take the idea and run with it, going into new territory. As the practice of PIEs continued to grow and evolve, become more widespread and more confident, so the ideas were being revised and adapted, to keep pace with emerging new developments. For this reason - and others besides - we needed eventually to expand the range of the phrase; and this is how the account we call 'PIEs 2.0' came about.

We'll go into this history in more detail later, as this continuing co-evolution of ideas and practice may help to explain some of the challenges in describing a developing picture. But the key point here is that this was, from the start, an evolving, exploratory approach, one of 'learning by doing'. It probably needs to continue to be so.

PIEs and 'Trauma Informed Care'

The practice of PIEs that has since developed in the UK is similar in many respects to a very similar approach emerging around the same time in the United States - which is as you might expect, because many services there were also meeting and responding creatively to the much same needs, in much the same context.

In both we see the same shared awareness that when people have fallen through the various safety nets that any society may have, and then find themselves homeless, there will have been many missed opportunities on the way. When homelessness services are engaging people who are often reluctant to seek help, and even distrustful of authorities and care givers, it's then important to make every contact count.

In the US the term suggested to describe this more integrated work was 'Trauma Informed Care' or 'TIC' - although in truth many of the developments being described in services were originally based not on any theoretical understanding of the psychology or neuroscience of trauma. Instead they grew from more values-based and humanitarian principles, and it was an intuitive understanding that paved the way for such more empathic responses, just as in the UK, where such development in services was largely grounded in ordinary emotional intelligence and intuitive understanding.

But what both were finding was that the more dynamic and inventive of social housing services were creating whole environments, in which everything was working towards maximising the potential for engagement and growth. We have since spent much of the next 10 -20 years working to identify quite what that means.

Bridging divides

Meanwhile, the PIE concept is proving to be remarkably dynamic. Like the services it describes, it's been constantly developing, learning and reaching out. Even the core idea of a PIE has evolved and is still evolving, in a continuous process of dialogue between 'the ideas people' and the services themselves, exploring these ideas in their day-to-day practice.

For example, when first we began talking about using the built environment 'and its social spaces' and opportunities, we had been thinking originally of the environment in a hostel, refuge, day centre or whatever buildings we had and managed. But we soon found that much the same awareness applies when approaching an individual in their own space, whether that be a flat of their own, a bedspace, or even just a patch of cardboard in a doorway.

This new thinking on where we may find these opportunities then became the bridge between the skills of engagement in 'shelter' and those in street outreach and in support at home, such as we saw emerging in Housing First and comparable programmes of 'housing-related support'. It is this key feature - the creation of and/or respect for the whole environment of the service or network of services - that became fundamental to the approach developing in the United Kingdom.

We do find that the term PIE captures rather better that key issue of an integrated overall effort, rooted in the spaces - of all kinds - that we can use. PIE is a rather broader term, and as we will see later, it allows us to tease out more of the key features in practical, operational terms; and it allows us to take into account the wider environment, the 'eco-system of service' in which all the efforts of any one service are entangled. It allows us to make links with other contexts and other ways of working with other equally complex needs.

So now we have a virtuous circle. Our understanding of PIEs has evolved and matured over these ten years or more into a fairly detailed programme of self-development for services. In the rest of this book, we will now try to tease out what that looks like in practice: where we can go with it; and how we can keep the freshness and dynamism, the respect for action learning, as the idea grows. There are always new, exciting, sometimes 'cutting edge' developments to describe. This is why the flexibility of a website, with its scope for changing content, its interactive forums and webinars etc. is so useful.

But there's one more thing to add from the start.

'Formative evaluation'

Later we will be looking more closely at the tools we have developed: the PIElink website itself, the PIEs framework and the Pizazz process. You will often hear it said that working as a PIE is more a journey than a destination. These tools are there to help you on the journey; and these all take a particular approach to recognition, evaluation and development that is known technically as 'formative evaluation'.

Formative evaluation is an on-going process, feeding back to any service or project where you seem to have reached, in whatever goals you may have have set. But with formative evaluation, the feedback comes not at the end, as a judgement or score, but throughout, as you continue to develop. It's like having a compass, or perhaps a backpack with the resources you need with you.

As we see it, developing as a PIE is a continuous process anyway - more a journey than a destination - and this means that you don't have to tackle all the issues thoroughly, in depth, from the start. In fact, practically nobody does everything, nor need anyone feel obliged to. They do what matters to them, in their situation.

It also means that you don't have to feel obliged to go any faster or any further than you feel ready to. You can go as far as you find useful, at any point in time. If it's a journey, take breaks. So for those just getting started on the road, besides the general advice here on introducing this approach, in the chapter on developing PIEs we will have a few encouraging comments on it being OK to be just 'a little bit PIE'd'.

You are already on your way

If you find the 'journey' metaphor works for you, you might think of this book as a kind of hitch-hiker's guide; the PIElink as a map, or a collection of maps; the PIEs framework as a set of co-ordinates by which to chart your journey; and the Pizazz as a way of checking the distance travelled, and how far you have still to go. But the destination you choose is your own.

CHAPTER FOUR

WHAT IS THE PIELINK?

You will have already noticed that we can't get even this far in an introduction to PIEs without repeatedly mentioning the PIElink (www.pielink.net), the dedicated on-line resource for 'all things PIE'. This next chapter therefore, aims to describe that website and what it aims to do, with its multiple pages, resources library, and forums.

Keeping it live

The PIEs idea was received with some enthusiasm when first it was suggested, and promptly endorsed in government guidance documents. But as the full potential and dynamism of this idea has become clear, it is important that it stays fresh, and open to developments. This is one more reason why a website, which can be constantly updated, is more use than a guidance document - even if, being rather complex, the site then needs some introduction with a guide like this.

With its many pages of advice, reflection and examples, and its members library, covering all aspects of the PIEs approach and open to the future, the PIElink was created to be a resource. But in the era of live streaming, we can now go even further. With active and interactive discussion 'forums', the PIElink is now growing into a key role as the online home for a growing community of practice.

When like-minded individuals meet face-to-face in the same localities, or in the same circles of specialist conferences and events, there is a depth to these contacts which can foster a real sense of common ground and partnership between agencies. Yet such meetings can at times be inhibited by wariness and unease over too much honesty, and this is often exacerbated by current approaches to funding that set out to create competition, which discourages open sharing of effective and emerging new practice.

By contrast, when community members can meet on line, although only in 2D, their geographical spacing means that this inhibiting divisiveness may often be almost entirely irrelevant. Shared and interactive learning from each other in real time conversation online may then bring a sense of camaraderie and a freedom that face-to-face meetings may lack.

Like any on-line community, the PIElink as a community of practice site is then something to draw support from, to contribute to, even to belong to. But it is also entirely optional, and members may be involved as much or as little as they wish to be with the various opportunities to participate in conversations, webinars and so on.

A resource library

Other than this, a website allows many more links and therefore many routes to much more of the discussion of issues than any book can offer. Footnotes in a book such as this can be a useful way to extend the main content, but endless references in footnotes or buried in the text can simply clog up the pages of a book. In any case, much of the most engaging content is in video form, which a book cannot show. Hyperlinks, written as text that you cannot click on, would be simply frustrating.

This is one reason why a book on PIEs is best devised as the companion to the website, where much of the most useful content is stored. The other reason is that this is a huge and complex subject; and the PIElink is a complex website. It is, in truth, a web. There is plenty to browse; but it's hard to know where to start, and easy to get lost; and some of the most interesting material, most relevant to any particular query, can simply get overlooked.

So for each of the main sections of this book there is now a corresponding page on the website, to help you go further. Many chapters even have pages with the same title, which should help. These should give a reliable and up-to-date account of many particular issues touched on in the chapters here, to follow up any issues you wish to explore more with links, examples and further discussion.

But a community of practice website is an organic, growing thing. We cannot entirely guarantee that the pages listed here will always remain in exactly their current shape, or place. Still, with the range of links we can now put there, you can be fairly sure of finding whatever you may be looking for.

Navigating the PIElink - a tour guide

With the ambition for a single framework for such a huge range of diverse services and approaches, there is a huge amount of ground to cover just in the PIEs concept itself, let alone all the illustrations and practice examples.

With a website on such a rich and complex subject, there are so many possible angles, weaving and inter-weaving, each of them just a click away, that we don't even try, on the site itself, to suggest one straight and 'recommended' channel. In consequence, on first encounter the design and layout of the website can seem to be quite a maze. It's certainly not a very conventional site; and this is one reason why we are now producing this handy guide, to help those new to it to find their way.

To get started, you might want to go straight to the Big Picture of PIEs 2.0, with '*Five Core Themes*', the overall themes and fifteen more specific practice elements, and follow any lead from there to the more specific features of PIEs 2.0, or to any more cross-cutting issues.

Nevertheless, for the PIElink we have now introduced two new and particularly useful features, the '*Quick Links*', and the '*Hot topics*'. The '*Quick Links*' can take you direct to some of the issues of particular interest to many. The '*Hot Topics*' take you to some of the most current discussions.

The 'START HERE!' page

So for all those entirely new to the whole idea of a PIE and to the site, it's a good idea to begin with one of the '*Quick Links*' pages there that has the same heading as this sub-section: '*START HERE!*'. It's in capitals - so you really can't miss it.

That page aims to offer new readers a sound general introduction; and from that page, through the website's multiple links design, you can then go straight to any of the other pages that interest you in particular, just as you wish. But to help you get started, here's some other suggestions.

For a broader introduction to the spirit of the PIE approach, you might browse the *'Some general advice'* page. It echoes the pages on this here in this book, but now with many more links to follow up whatever aspect interests you.

In *'Developing PIEs'* you will find a section specifically on *'Introducing the PIE approach'*, which matches that chapter of this book. Here we start to look at the issues of going at the pace that suits you; and from 2023 we are hosting a regular live and interactive forum on *'Setting Up Services'*. It's likely to prove a favourite, and become a regular feature.

So for those with quite specific interests and concerns - which is probably most people - by using the main tabs and menus on the Home page and the *'Quick Links'* you can often go straight to the topic, area or subject that drew you here in the first place, to make your way in.

Otherwise on various pages we have specific examples, in writing or in video form, of services that have taken steps - in some cases their very first steps - on this journey. In each case, on each page of topics there is a wealth of hyperlinks, to take you further down any path you want to follow.

For those who would like at this stage to browse a selection of these examples, you will now find here the links to all the *'Case studies and practice examples'* - some of which we will also include here, on the concluding pages of this introduction. From there with just one click you can find, view or read and download accounts of any more quite specific examples of practice on the issues you want to explore.

The members' library

Besides these quite general introductions, a host of pages discussing particular aspects or applications of the ideas and practice and the collections of practice examples, there are other gems to be found in the members' library.

In the library in particular you find many more resources, with a wide selection of the most useful items we can find, ranging from government guidance to 1-1 conversations, articles, published papers, audio files, specially produced video content and webinar presentations and training materials - even cartoons - all for the purpose of sharing experience and practice, research, thoughts and opinions.

The library is a curated collection; that is to say, we have done our best to find and select those items that we felt were most helpful, most relevant. But there are new publications coming on stream all the time; and many of them we do not even spot. Inclusion of only a small selection here does not mean that those not included are not perhaps equally relevant.

All the items in the library are freely given away, but note: only to registered members. The reason to restrict access to members is partly that these are sometimes the terms we have agreed with the authors of some articles, for their inclusion here. Where papers were produced by others, many were already in the public domain and free, but in some case we have sought the express permission of the authors and publishers to share them here.

But an even better reason to register is that when people register, we get to hear from them a little about who it is that is interested in these ideas; and we get a chance to ask them what is most helpful to them, and what else we might explore.

Forums, webinars and Special Interest Groups

Finally, registering members give us permission to contact them with news and invitations to on-line events, such as webinars and - now that we are all accustomed to interactive live streaming - the forums that we held via Zoom beginning in 2021; and mean to develop in future as a key resource.

One of the central ambitions for the PIElink was that it should be not just a resource library for services developing as PIEs, but a host for other active, engaged networks - the home of a community of practice.

It took a while for the technology to realise that ambition to become commonplace, but one of the most welcome developments of 2021 - there weren't many, after all, in the second year of the COVID epidemic - was the way it suddenly became quite normal to use video conferencing and chats with colleagues and family. This is where the community of practice ambition for the website now comes most into its own.

Future proofing: the once and future PIElink

if you are reading these words, then you have in your hands a first edition copy of 'Psychologically Informed Environments from the ground up'. This means that the person who purchased it - it may have been you? - was an early adopter; and is surely to be congratulated for that.

But it also means that over time, as the PIEs idea grows and evolves, some of the vocabulary we use may be modified in responding to address new issues; the sections, their page names and locations on the PIElink that we describe here may have moved on. We do at least anticipate that there will be a new design for the Home page, with a more contemporary styling - more suited to mobile phones, for example.

In any case, one of the risks in creating any users' manual or handbook for any kind of software or software-related (ie. webinar and web-based) 'product' is the likelihood that the manual will begin to slip out of date as soon as the next revision of the software is introduced.

However, in the last few months up to the Summer of 2023 a thorough review of the PIElink has been undertaken, with a number of significant changes and re-designs of the page structure. The new design aims to ensure that the website remains 'backwards compatible' with the book.

Backwards compatibility

For example, the re-design to introduce '*Quick Links*' such as the '*START HERE!*' page and '*Hot Topics*' will allow the flexibility to develop new areas of interest incrementally, without compromising the current structure. These, or something recognisably similar, are very likely to be in any new site design.

All the main features of the PIEs framework will also be immediately accessible, via the Homepage; and the guidance on developing as PIEs, including the advice on introducing the PIE approach into services where it is now yet known. Advice on using the Pizazz, whether on paper or with the PIE Abacus software, should also be immediately accessible.

As we will see in the next chapter, that same principle of backwards compatibility has been followed in the revision of the earlier accounts of what makes for a PIE, to develop and expand PIEs One into PIEs 2.0.

Forwards compatibility

Finally, we have introduced a whole new section for the growing range of '*PIE publications*', which you can now access via the *Quick Links*. Here we have a sub-section specifically for this book, with further pages to match each chapter; and other publications to follow.

Here we can suggest more of the library items or areas on the site that touch on the issues discussed in chapters of this book - some that may not be obvious, and easily overlooked. That's often where the really interesting finds are.

But even more valuably, here we can keep the book itself up to speed with new developments and new content. Where a more conventional book can only offer a references section, and even an e-book can only provide links to specific content at the point of publication, this innovative linkage of a book and a website can introduce the reader to an on-going conversation that they can then be part of.

Certainly there may one day be a second edition of this book, more faithfully reflecting in future the language and page locations of the PIEs approach, as it continues to evolve. In the meantime, the structure and the content are now fully up-to date - or as up-to-date as any picture of a constantly evolving world of practice can be - and all the material mentioned here will remain in place on the website, and will still be accessible via any new design.

Taking inspiration from others

At this point, to round off this introduction, it would be helpful to take a look at a few actual examples to illustrate the issues that we have attempted to sum up as the work of PIEs. But selecting just a few examples to illustrate the PIEs approach in practice here is difficult.

With such breadth, it really isn't possible to give just a handful of examples of the thinking in action that we tried to sum up firstly in the idea of a PIEs, and later in the fully developed PIEs framework. It is just too varied, and most examples are quite specific to their particular context. A very small selection can be misleading.

The two UK government guidance documents on homelessness that first spoke of psychologically informed services and PIEs (in 2010 and 2012) each did include a dozen or more examples of the work being done in some services, to illustrate the kind of responsive creativity they wanted to encourage. These are still available on the PIElink, via the Case studies and practice examples pages.

Since then we have amassed many more examples on the PIElink, and for a much wider range of services and needs. This is where the website is so much more useful than any book can aim to be; and this section of the book probably the least satisfactory on its own. But here is where having the synergy between a book and the website and its library with its videos, audio file and other links becomes most useful.

Complexity and categories

Categorising these examples by just one feature is always difficult and potentially unhelpful because, as we have suggested, these services tend to be multi-faceted. In addition, many of the early examples did not use the term PIE, as it had not then been coined; and many good services, especially outside the UK, may well recognise their work in the description here, but have not yet come across the term.

On the PIElink's pages these examples tend to be shown (via links) in relation to each particular topic being discussed - although many, of course, will be examples of more than one thing (and in any case, most would be far too modest to describe themselves as exemplary).

On the PIElink the search function may be useful; but all such searches of websites with a huge library store tend to give odd selections, and this is as true of the PIElink as of any other. We have also attempted some broad clustering of examples, grouped according to the likely interests of services working in particular settings, which may be helpful, although it is incomplete at best, and always out of date.

At the time of going to print, the clusters there are:

- Introducing the PIE approach
- The built environment and adaptations
- Using the whole environment
- Outreach, pathways, environments without buildings
- PIEs, communities and a sense of belonging
- Clubhouses, cores, and campus models
- PIEs in therapy settings
- 'Psychologically informed business environments'
- Whole system PIEs
- PIEs and 'exclusion-informed research'

Another small selection of case studies and examples

Here therefore we will give a handful of examples, more to illustrate the breadth of the territory than to go into any depth. Via the *Case Studies and practice examples* pages, and on the pages on particular practice topics, you will find these and a great deal more.

But if some of these already whet your appetite to look up some specific stories or analyses, do feel free to pause at any point, go to that page on the site itself, and start to check out the links to each item in the PIElink library.

Meanwhile, since the PIElink already groups examples by setting and by topics, for this selection let us take another approach again, and here we will group them by:

* Design or re-design of buildings and services
* Techniques for engagement and a sense of belonging
* Thinking differently

In almost all cases, each example in each category here could just as well have appeared in another; or in all three. These clusters are just one way to start exploring.

Designing buildings and services

- **Opening spaces: Simon Community Access Hub, Glasgow.** After attending a workshop on PIEs, the team at the Simon Community in Glasgow began completely rethinking the reception area for their city-centre street drop in for rough sleepers. Here is an example of relationship-centred practice, radically changing the built environment, and also encouraging partnership and co-location of services.

- **'No magnolia anywhere': The Wallich, Cardiff.** This staff briefing on using the PIE ideas on the built environment was prepared as a briefing for the team at a specific hostel in the Wallich's group. The images are sufficiently anonymised to be shared; and the overall advice and approach - eg: to 'walk through the building' - is widely applicable.
- **Elastic tolerance and the impact of low-cost changes: Highwater House, Norwich.** The annual report for Highwater House describes the impact of changes introduced after attending a PIE workshop. It shows the synergies in the PIEs approach, in using elastic tolerance, finding low cost changes in the use of the rooms: developing a move-on service, and co-location.
- **Working with limited strengths and short time spans: The Big Issue, London.** In *'The Big Issue as a psychologically informed business environment'* Stephen Robertson, CEO, describes the carefully structured opportunities that selling the magazine creates. Here is an example of a 'psychologically informed business environment', consciously working with short attention spans and fragile ambitions, as a kind of 'scaffolding of engagement' to cater for weaknesses and allow new strengths to develop.
- **Short time spans and person-centred incentives: Potter Street hostel, Mansfield.** In *'Banking on Time'*, Graham Gardiner describes devising inventive ways of working with the meagre budgets of a supported accommodation unit, working with short attention span of his service users, in a person-centred approach: and so creating in miniature a 'PIE business environment'.

- **Tackling the leaving care crisis: Social Services Dept, Haringey.** An account of the re-designing of a residential care adolescent's unit in the 1970s to cater for young people facing the crisis of independence created by 'leaving care' using a clubhouse or 'core-and cluster' approach.
- **A trauma informed design (TID) checklist: Design Resources for Homelessness, Florida.** Amongst many other useful resources for building design and adaptation, Jill Pable of Design Resources for Homelessness has created a checklist for a trauma-informed approach to the physical environment of a building.
- **Forgivable loans: 1011 Lansdowne, Toronto:** Here Elise Hug describes some of the creative thinking, especially on partnerships in funding that lay behind the redevelopment of a run-down tower block in Toronto. This is a chapter taken - with permission, of course - from another collection of case studies, the ebook on Housing First in Canada, *Exploring Effective Systems Responses to Homelessness*.
- **System change and system brokers: Fulfilling Lives, Newcastle and Gateshead.** Ray Middleton & Alex Smith describe attempts at tackling barriers and dysfunctional relationships between agencies by working closely with a group of those most excluded, in order to learn from individual experiences. Here is person-centred system brokerage specifically intended as providing information for wider system change.

Engagement and a sense of belonging

- **'The biscuits are important': Focus Ireland, Cork.** Ger Spillane of Focus Ireland offices, Cork; on the tiny things that help in creating a relaxed and accepting atmosphere.
- **The democracy of pidgin: Aux Captifs la Liberation, Paris.** Some observations on the power of simple language in a day centre meeting both practical and emotional needs with a loose-knit, accepting community, and 'the strength of weak ties'.
- **The engagement window and the safe couch: Right There, West Kirkbride.** Modest changes to the furnishings and the built environment that change the experience for all concerned; another service for youngsters with a clubhouse model.
- **Community work on the streets: REACH, Western Massachusetts.** Brendan Plante of the outreach and assessment team in Western Massachusetts on pre-treatment, and just 'being there'.
- **Group support, clinical input and community with tenancy: 1811 Eastlake, Seattle.** Daniel Malone and colleagues outline 'congregated' or 'single site' housing for an actively supportive recovery community in the US, working within the Housing First model. (This is an example of a PIE without knowing the name.)
- **Working together: ADAPT, West Sussex.** In *'Building recovery communities'* Brian Morgan tells the history of creating a peer support community for a group in recovery from addiction, as a small business; this is another example of developing 'a psychologically informed business environment'.

- **Images of home: research project, University of Plymouth.** Leonie Boland, an Occupational Therapist, describes an innovative research project using photography, and lateral thinking on what constitutes 'support'. Here tenants' own images, and the personal meanings they give to their own 'social spaces', help to appreciate and enrich their own efforts in making a new home.
- **Walking together: JustLife, Brighton.** The work of Temporary Accommodation Action Groups extends beyond service-to-service liaison; here they find ways of keeping in touch with those housed in temporary accommodation, who can get lost in the system, to maintain 'social connection' without treating them as 'service users'.

Thinking differently

- **The meaning of reception: Pole Rosa Luxembourg, Paris. 'L'acceuil'** - *Reception, welcome and acceptance:*' Claude Chevrier in an address (in French, translated) to a psychoanalytic colloquium, on rethinking the complex emotional and social meanings of 'reception' at a homelessness accommodation unit in the 13e arrondisement
- **Rethinking the staff role: University of Hertfordshire.** *'The scaffolding of hope'* is a psychology degree dissertation on a study of men who had had multiple moves. Coral Westaway sees making relationships central to engagement, and emphasises the relational nature of hope. This entails seeing the staff role in a new light; another example of PIE thinking arising from exclusion-informed research.

- **Noticing small things: an outreach worker's blog, Stoke on Trent.** *'My car is a psychologically informed environment'*: Ruth Franceska's blog describes noticing a subtle change when using her car as part of her outreach work to ferry someone to an appointment.
- **Appreciative Inquiry at King George's Hostel: London.** *'Back on your feet'* is a short film, accompanied by two published articles, with Suzanne Quinney describing a pilot for using Appreciative Inquiry as a strengths model: an example of user co-production in developing a 'learning organisation'.
- **Exclusion-informed research: conference presentation, London.** Juliette Hough and Becky Rice, in a workshop presentation identifying some key operational principles for person-centred and exclusion-informed research.
- **Power imbalance and empowerment techniques: Participatory Appraisal, Tower Hamlets.** Zack Ahmed describes adopting a novel approach for 'local area systems learning' in a public health consultation with substance abuse service users, using an approach derived from post-colonial community development to correct the imbalance in power relationships: this is exclusion-informed community development research.
- **Introducing reflective practice on psychiatric wards: NHS, Bristol.** *'Towards a PIE city'* is a presentation by psychologist Sian Clark on applying PIEs and psychology in acute psychiatry wards in Bristol; on the value of reflective practice: and the potential for application of PIEs in hospitals and other therapy settings.

- **'TCs' and the emergence of a new social psychiatry.** *'In search of the enabling environment'* is an M.A. degree dissertation essay on rethinking the contemporary nature and legacy of the therapeutic community. (NB: This is the precursor to the paper that launched the phrase PIE, some thirty years later.)
- **'Commissioning for complexity': the need for new thinking on funding frameworks.** In *'A Whole New World'*, Toby Lowe and his colleagues at Collaborate and Human Learning Systems outline a radically different approach to the commissioning of public services, to allow for trust and dialogue between funders and providers. This is the PIE approach at funding and strategic level, or 'systemic PIE', promoting 'a PIE of pathways' (sic): and creating markers of 'whole systems change'.

FIVE CORE THEMES

Getting into the details with the PIEs framework

The PIE idea is a way of seeing your work, and seeing it as a whole. So far in this account we have concentrated on the spirit that we found underlying and underpinning many of the developments that we saw; and we could only describe and illustrate this in practice with a few dozen examples. But at some point it becomes more helpful to attempt to tease out some underlying themes. This is what the PIEs framework aims to do.

We do find that the core elements of the framework work best when taken all together. This is a 'holistic' model, and there is a synergy between these parts, so that the whole is bigger. That's why we needed to find a framework and a process that can look at this whole in practical terms, and from many different angles.

This is not to say that all these elements will always be found in all services. There is some advice on 'being a little bit PIE'd', that we discuss in the next chapter. But we do find that most of it is relevant - if not always to what you are working on now, then sometimes to what you may need to work on next.

'PIEs One' : the first full account

As the ideas and the practice here continued to grow and to evolve over the second decade of the 21st Century, one formulation of what we might mean by a PIE began to come together. This is the version that we therefore now call 'PIEs One' - the original (or sometimes 'the classic') account.

Although the actual wording used may vary in slightly different versions of this earliest account (from circa 2013-16), in PIEs One the main or 'headline' features of a PIE are five:

- Seeing relationships as central to all successful work
- Seeing support for staff, too, as important
- Using a psychological 'model' or framework
- Using the built environment ('and its social spaces') to maximum effect
- Gathering and sharing evidence of effectiveness (or 'evidence-generating')

There is however a sixth key feature, always included but not always given its own headline, which is 'encouraging reflective practice'.

As an account of what we saw within services, this proved very popular. Yet as the idea spread and evolved, some limitations in the scope of this earlier version gradually became clear. After a few more years, work began to update this with a second version, which we therefore called 'PIEs 2.0,' using the analogy of software up-dates.

One important principle in this 'up-date' was that the new version should be, in software language, 'backwards compatible' - that is, that all the features of the original version should be included, recognisable and usable in the new, while the 'bugs' were sorted out, and 'new functionality' was added.

PIEs 2.0: an expanded range of issues

With PIEs 2.0, we also have five 'top level' themes, but they cover a broader canvas. These top five areas are:

- Developing more 'psychological awareness' of the needs of service users and staff
- Valuing training and support for staff (and others, including volunteers) as well as service users.
- Creating a service philosophy (or 'culture') of continuous 'learning and enquiry'
- Creating and/or working with 'spaces of opportunity'
- Fine-tuning 'the 3 Rs' - the rules, roles and overall responsiveness of the service

In PIEs 2.0, in each of these five main themes we then down into fifteen more specific 'practice elements', which focus on the more tangible or more practical expressions of each of those five wider themes. It may help to see these two formulations compared side by side, to spot the areas that have been expanded with these practice elements. The themes in PIEs One are shown here with asterisks.

PSYCHOLOGICAL AWARENESS
Emotional awareness (aka active empathy)
Engagement approaches and techniques
Psychological model(s) *

STAFF TRAINING & SUPPORT*
Staff training
Staff support

LEARNING & ENQUIRY
Reflective practice * and action learning
Developing a culture of enquiry
Evidence-generating practice*
Sector engagement

SPACES OF OPPORTUNITY
The built environment and its social spaces*
Surroundings and networks
Pathways and systems coherence

THE THREE R's (='*making relationships central*' *)
The day-to-day operating procedures of the service
Available staff and user roles created in the service
Responsiveness – the flexibility of the service

At this stage in exploring the PIE approach, we need only note that almost all the issues identified in PIEs One are still there, in the PIEs 2.0 framework. The only exception is the centrality of relationships; and that is because in PIEs 2.0, it is central. It's simply everywhere.

The main point in showing this evolution is that the responsiveness, flexibility and adaptability that we expect to see in PIEs can be reflected in the same flexibility in the PIEs framework, and in the way it is used. These two versions each have different strengths, and when introducing these ideas it's quite possible to start with PIEs One, and up-grade only later, when wanting to get more practical and operational.

But we'll save a more extended discussion of the relative strengths of each for the following chapter, on introducing the PIEs approach in services. Since all but one of these key features of a PIE identified in PIEs One are included in the expanded version, we will spell them all out here; and then come back to look at the differences and strengths of each.

Working with the practice elements

Closer and more specific to operational practice than the five big themes in the PIE framework, the meaning in context of these 'elements' will need to be interpreted, adjusted or 'customised' to the needs of the specific service - the client group, the nature of the service, the geography of the locality, the language and technical terms that are more suited to your particular work.

So, for example, by 'built environment' in different contexts you might take this to mean the look of the building, the lighting and signage in the reception area; or it might mean using a local park or coffee bar as a place to meet; or even being careful about how you step into someone else's space, whether that is a bedroom or a patch of carpet in a doorway.

PSYCHOLOGICAL AWARENESS

We have described a psychologically informed environment as 'one that takes into account the psychological make-up – the thinking, emotions, personalities and past experience – of its participants, in the way it operates.' But let's look a little closer now at what that might cover; and how, with the PIEs 2.0 framework, that can be translated into operational practice.

Active empathy

The first element here - and by far the most necessary – is the one we simply call empathy, or 'psychological' or perhaps 'emotional intelligence'. This is the 'psychology' that we all have and use, just as human beings. That broader 'psychological awareness' or 'emotional intelligence' is the bedrock on which a PIE is built; and for many services, it can be sufficient to create the level of responsiveness that creates a PIE. Certainly without it, nothing else will.

In the PIEs 2.0 framework, we see 'psychological awareness' as potentially operating at any level within any service - 'from top to toe' and beyond, extending into the networks, pathways and systems that we have created which, as we'll see, can also be more 'psychologically informed'.

Approaches and techniques

The second element is the use of general approaches or particular techniques, many of which might be usefully drawn from 'psychology', in a more technical sense. Much of this can be taught, though much of what we do is still intuitive. Shaking hands, making eye contact when someone walks in, finding the right words to use – these are things we all just do. Still, there are many new things we can yet learn, and there are many examples of particular techniques on the website.

NB: In the PIEs framework, we treat both Trauma-Informed Care and Housing First as 'approaches'. Trauma itself is of course a psychological model; but TIC is the operational response - an approach, but one with many forms of expression.

Adopting a psychological model

The third element is the option of adoption within a service of a particular 'psychological model' such as CBT, or psychodynamic thinking, to shape and guide many or all aspects of the services' work. It is sometimes thought that a 'psychological model' is necessary for any service, to call itself a PIE. But really it only needs to be whatever you feel you need, to understand the people you work with. (In short: don't make it any more complicated than it needs to be.)

It is for this reason that PIEs 2.0, and the Pizazz, the PIEs self-assessment process - which we come to later - both use the term 'psychological awareness', rather than 'psychological model', as the overall theme for this whole aspect of any service's PIE approach. This will allow a service to rate itself quite freely, even perhaps quite positively, on 'active empathy', without any use of any specific techniques or models at all.

But before we leave the theme of psychological awareness, we should spare a thought for those that work in or manage any of these services. It is not just the psychological and emotional needs of your service users that you must attend to. Staff and colleagues are people too, with psychological and emotional needs that must be recognised.

In practical terms, we will look at how an agency supports its staff in the next item in this chapter; and again in the following section, on cultivating an attitude of learning and enquiry, when challenges arrive - as they will surely do.

TRAINING AND SUPPORT

Granted what we now understand better of the emotional complexity that many in homelessness and similar services for complex needs may be facing, working as a PIE suggests having a far greater focus on the wear and tear that this work can entail. Certainly one of the features of the PIE approach that seemed to go down particularly well, when it was first spelled out in PIEs One, was the insistence that staff too needed support.

For PIEs 2.0 we separate the specific key practice elements in the 'Training and Support' theme into two: training, and support. We will address them in turn; but then we will have a little more to add on how they work together.

Training needs

By training we suggest that, beyond basic induction into the procedures of any service, covering health and safety and recording keeping etc, the staff will typically benefit from training in understanding all the particular issues that the service users group may be facing.

This is not just about psychological and emotional issues, but the practical challenges and barriers many face, and in the 'sector engagement' element of 'Learning and Enquiry', we will look at how pro-active involvement with other services in the locality can help educate all services in how best to work together, to improve such 'pathways' between services.

Nevertheless, a minimal understanding at least of psychological and emotional trauma is likely to be helpful to all staff - not just to those in services explicitly for people with 'complex needs'; and not just for the 'frontline ' staff, who have the immediate and direct encounters with their 'users'.

There is a lot of material on trauma and TIC; so on the relevant pages on the PiElink, we have focussed on a small selection particularly relevant to this way of thinking. Otherwise, there is no 'core curriculum' that is expected or required, for services to 'be a PIE'. It's all entirely down to the work you are doing.

But in any case, not all training takes the form of sitting in a room with others and being shown Powerpoint slides or given exercises. Much learning is 'on the job' training (technically called 'experiential' learning).

Support needs

By 'staff support' we mean a pervasive and pro-active attitude within any organisation and a wide range of ways to look after the needs of staff, not just making available counselling for staff who are particularly struggling. There are so many ways to meet staff needs that it may not be particularly helpful to list them, even as examples.

It may be worth noting that some of the earliest published reports on the use of the Pizazz self-assessment process to develop services have found that it seemed to bring benefits for staff morale. It seems that being listened to, and given some scope for leading on developments in services, was good for staff morale and welfare.

Not just paid staff

By 'staff', however, we may mean not solely the payroll staff, the employees, but all those who contribute to the creation and functioning of a service, including volunteers, and especially those service users who take on any constructive role. (This aspect of the 2.0 model - giving thought to the roles available to staff, users and others - is explored more under the broader theme of 'The Three R's'.)

What else counts as support?

Finally, support is not just a 1-1, face-to-face issue. It shows in the attitude of the whole agency to responding to problems, extending to the way it may respond officially to any problems that staff may experience. Some services are reviewing their HR policies, to be better aligned with the PIE approach.

Encouraging reflective practice can also help develop an atmosphere within a team that respects and supports the day-to-day experience of being a worker; and can help resolve disagreements or dilemmas over the management of particular incidents or of changes in working practice.

A culture of enquiry in the organisation as a whole then provides the essential supportive learning environment, with reflective practice in whatever form as one of the key approaches. In the next section in this chapter, on 'Learning and Enquiry', we will look at the way reflective practice is also being used as one key element among others to help sharpen any agency's response to the demands of the service, and to understand what, as an agency, it may need to be doing.

Not just your own staff?

There are also some services that have found that to do their job, they need to train or 'raise the awareness' not just of their own staff, but that of others they must work with. Every encounter with a colleague from another agency or service is an opportunity to advocate and explain.

Where some services have taken on this task with real enthusiasm and commitment, we are starting to go beyond the word 'training' and to verge on some of the issues we will encounter next, in what we call 'sector engagement' - one of the practice elements in the 'Learning and Enquiry' theme, coming up next.

LEARNING AND ENQUIRY

The 'Psychological Awareness' theme is all about how the service understands both its services users and its staff. The 'Learning and Enquiry' theme, by contrast, is about how the agency understands itself. In the PIEs 2.0 account, learning and enquiry describes an attitude, a frame of mind within an organisation or service as a whole.

This can be expressed in many ways. Here we try to cover all the main ways in which the organisation itself tries to understand what it does, and what it needs to be doing.

Embedding a 'culture of enquiry'

Creating a 'culture of enquiry' means adopting an attitude and an atmosphere of wanting to learn from difficulties, whether specific incidents, or from general shifts in the needs and the demands on the service. The opposite of a culture of enquiry might then be a culture of blame - whether blaming the client or the staff or others. But equally, it might mean a culture of unquestioning adherence to the rules, or the terms of the funding contract.

In the live and interactive forum discussion programme that ran through the whole of 2021, one subject that came up repeatedly was the need to 'embed' the PIE way of thinking 'from top to toe' throughout the whole of an organisation that wishes its services to work as PIEs.

As these conversations continued, it became clear that this embedding was not just a vertical integration issue - infusing these ideas from top to bottom of the single organisation. It might equally involve talking with partner agencies working in the same locality to understand each other better; and with funders over what they thought they wanted from the services that they fund.

When we come, later in this book, to discuss self-assessment of your services using the Pizazz assessment and development process, your teams' analysis of what helps and hinders can also address what is missing in the local system as a whole. This may then be valuable feedback for local managers, funders and commissioners over more 'systemic' constraints, developing a culture of enquiry in the whole system.

Encouraging reflective practice

Much of the consistent feedback from services over the past few years has been that encouraging reflective practice can often be a most effective way to develop as a PIE. It can help to truly embed the PIEs approach in the working of the service, from the ground up. This is why in some versions of the PIEs One account, it may be given a headline of its own, as a sixth theme.

Reflective practice can take many forms, from individual to team to the whole organisation. But as we mean it here, when reflective practice is shared, in teams, it seems to do most to establish the attitude of a culture of enquiry, and to translate thinking with emotional intelligence into practical responses.

On the whole, reflective practice in services will often focus on a specific recent event, perhaps an example of an untoward incident where the team wants to share the experience in a supportive way or to explore any dilemmas or conflicts that might have been revealed. But it can be just as useful - and often less threatening to begin with, for those new to it - to look instead at something that went well, and see what the team can learn from that.

At its best, reflectiveness is not just something done in a group, in time set aside. It becomes part of the day-to-day culture of a service. But in services that are particularly keen to encourage reflection and learning from experience in 'frontline' services, putting time aside for team reflective practice sessions may be helpful.

There are differing views on how far it is helpful for involvement in such sessions to be emphasised, or even made compulsory for team members to attend. The one thing we can suggest is that if it is to be compulsory, there should be a clear rationale for doing so, in terms of the needs of the user group; and that that rationale can be clearly communicated - and questioned.

Sector engagement

A culture of learning and enquiry, rather than of adherence and blame, can also operate at the level of whole systems, local partnerships and pathways. The systems change and 'system brokerage' efforts we have seen in many areas are examples of system-level learning and enquiry. We call this element in the PIEs 2 framework 'sector engagement'.

This might for example mean positive encouragement of staff to attend local forums to discuss needs: 'mapping and gapping' exercises. Here we are really asking about how much opportunity there is for the staff and the users of any service to get actively involved in improving the coherence of the local eco-system of services; and how far they feel listened to, if they do.

Evidence-generating practice

For those that can make the time, being involved with research is very helpful, not just for the new knowledge that it creates, but for the feeling that it conveys that the work you do actually matters, and the issues taken seriously.

The earliest accounts of a PIE had sometimes attempted to suggest that 'evidence generating practice' or 'evaluating outcomes' might be seen as a hallmark of a 'proper' PIE. But depending on how this is taken, it may seem a lot to ask; and this suggestion caused a good deal of unnecessary confusion.

Outcomes measurement clearly has a place here; but in recognising the complexity of people's underlying needs we may need to challenge any simplistic assessment of success, and the overall focus of research needs to be far broader than simply attempting to quantify the outcomes of complex interventions.

There certainly is a need for more research in the field of homelessness; and for more of a research-friendly culture in the sector. More formal research projects and agencies do therefore have a clear place in the new framework as a focus for their efforts. But being involved in formal research is fairly uncommon. 'Evidence generating' in the strictest sense of producing publishable research cannot really be seen as a yardstick for all PIEs.

By not making this element so central, by treating this possibility not as a core theme but somewhere further down in the list in the PIEs 2 framework, we meant to allow services to shine in the things that really matter to any service - the thoughtfulness of the agency in relation to service users and staff, the attempts to engage other services in understanding and backing your work.

So it's not that we want to discourage learning from what works; it's that we also want to see the data we need for this kind of research coming directly from the experience of the staff and users. In the chapters here on using the Pizazz self-assessment and service development process, especially with the PIE Abacus, the software version, we will touch on some of the ways this audit tool can perhaps be used in research.

SPACES OF OPPORTUNITY

The 'Spaces of Opportunity' theme is essentially about how users move through your service. It will probably come as no real surprise that when we think of services as 'psychologically informed environments', the actual physical environment(s) of the service - the layout, furnishings, signage, etc - was one of the main features to consider.

But we now recognise that we must go beyond simply considering the buildings we manage. 'Environment' is a very broad, very flexible term. It will mean different things in different contexts. (We will come back to this a little later in this book, in the section called 'What is 'an environment?'). So what exactly do we mean by using 'spaces' here? What aspects of the environment do we mean to include in this?

For the PIEs 2 framework we have expanded quite considerably the range that we may be able to consider under this general theme. All the ways to move through a service are included here, to cover all the possible pathways that service users move through - including, therefore, the extent to which these external pathways are themselves designed with service users' needs in mind.

In fact, we now suggest it's most useful in practice to distinguish three main areas or aspects (the 'practice elements') of the whole services environment:

- The built environment itself, and what we have called its 'social spaces', where things happen.
- The local surroundings and networks that any service works with, or within; the location, local facilities, and how you may use them to best effect.

- The referral routes and move-on options in which it operates, and the overall coherence (or lack of it) in this 'services eco-system': the systems and pathways.

These three are actually rather different kinds or aspects of this very broad concept, 'the environment'. Putting them all together under the same theme or headline then meant identifying what we might see as the common thread.

This, we suggest, is about the opportunities that the service can find, or can create, to engage their users and assist them in whatever progress they may make, or whatever path they may take. (Conversely, all these elements, if not well thought through, can limit or constrain the potential for users – and 'put them in their place'.) Hence the much broader general title - to treat all these as 'spaces of opportunity'.

A further note on 'social spaces'

Note also that here, even when talking of the actual built environment and the physical surroundings of a service, it is the 'social spaces' that can be created that give them their key meaning. By this we mean not just all the spaces that are designated as 'social', such as a shared kitchen, TV lounge or meetings rooms, but all those that have some emotional meaning, through the interactions that will happen there.

A waiting room or entrance lobby, for example, is laden with emotional significance, and so can be designed or adapted - at least furnished and lit - with an eye to how you hope people will be feeling when they first arrive. In the library you will find a couple of examples of ways to 'walk through' your buildings, to imagine how it might feel to someone new entering.

Working in other people's environments

It's worth mentioning here that even in street outreach work, your staff are working within a built environment; it's just not one over which you have any control. But still you must approach the spaces around those you encounter here with thoughtful respect. Even a square of cardboard is someone's space.

Similarly in a Housing First service, the key environment is the individual's own home; and how you may enter there, or not, is on their terms. You might also want to give thought to other places and ways to meet, such as a local park or coffee bar; or any sports or recreational space.

Here the 'social spaces' are those that arise in the interaction between people; and personal space is no less important, just because it has no obvious physical boundaries.

The wider services environment

It's probably only when we look more closely at each of these three kinds of space, and the ways of moving through a service in terms of the opportunities we can create, that we can fully see the value of widening the frame in this way, with not one but three kinds of 'movement through' to consider.

This is true especially of the systems and pathways in which services work, because it is the inclusion of this element that now allows services and their users to give their views on the wider eco-system of services, and any gaps and barriers; and then to share these experiences with others. This becomes particularly significant when we come later to look at the possibilities for developing local audit; and to include here service users' own collective assessments of local services.

THE THREE Rs (or Rules, Roles and Responsiveness)

The 'spaces' theme is essentially about how users move through your service; and they are clustered together, to cover all the pathways that service users move through. But in a complex world for complex needs, this division of the practice elements into five big themes could never be neat, and there is a lot of overlap. Referral procedures, for example, sit at the boundary between the procedures of one agency and the pathways into and through it.

We now recognise the importance of all these component parts to make a whole, for a well-integrated and responsive service. But there is one other whole cluster of features that are equally central to the opportunities that a service creates. These are the opportunities that are created by or within the rules and procedures of the services.

This is the inner environment of services. These are the areas of a services' work that are largely within the scope of the agency to adjust; and they are so important - and also sufficiently distinct - that in the end we concluded that we had to give them a cluster and a theme of their own: the rules, roles and responsiveness of the service, which become, conveniently, 'the Three Rs'.

The day-to-day work

We use the phrase 'the Three Rs' as a shorthand to focus on the key elements in the day-to-day running of any service. The psychological awareness that we bring, the training and support of staff, the spaces with which we work, all provide us with many opportunities to engage. But in making constructive relationships and in the framing of day-to-day encounters, it's the Three Rs that do most of the heavy lifting.

The Three Rs theme provides a tighter and more precise focus on the nitty gritty of the working life of services - the rules and procedures of the service, and that last harder to pin down element - how responsive the service can be.

The central place of working through relationships still runs through everything in the PIEs approach. But it does so most obviously, and most practically, in the Three Rs. The essential ingredients are (obviously) those three:

- the rules and procedures of the service, that govern the day-to-day operations - this is what in the army they call 'the rules of engagement'
- the roles that are available - for both staff and users - within the social structure
- and finally, the more un-written rules, the ways in which the service actually works - the responses or responsiveness to events.

This trio of rules, roles, and responsiveness aims to focus on the immediate and practical expressions of a service - what it actually does, and 'how it rolls': its operational procedures, as they affect the life and opportunities of the service users. This is where the centrality of relationships has most tangible impact.

The case studies, some of which we introduced earlier in that section on exploring the PIElink, have many examples of quite specific changes in operational practice, some with sweeping effect, some small but crucial. The significance and impact of such changes is often only identifiable in context.

It is for this reason that we argue that services and teams need to have the opportunity - and the freedom - to explore for themselves the real impact of the rules, roles and procedures - that they work by; and to do so in teams, with some of the tools that we have gathered or created, for the purpose.

The rules

The rules and procedures of a service will cover all aspects of the service that are set by the agency, as its established practice. We will naturally tend to be particularly interested in the procedures and rules that directly affect the service users and govern interactions with them - referral procedures, opening hours, care and support planning, access to specific areas of a building, sanctions or eviction procedures.

Sometimes procedures may arise from the ways the service is contracted, or funded, issues that are outside the service's or the agency's immediate control. Sometimes they may come centrally, from 'agency policy' that may not have kept pace with the ambition to be more 'psychologically informed'.

But sometimes there is scope for the procedures to be fine-tuned locally. Analysing thoughtfully the impact of these rules to see what might be remedied, can then be very fruitful, particularly in discussions with service users (and sometimes with other referring or move-on agencies).

A range of roles

A key part of the organisation of any services is the range of roles for both staff and service users that are available and that allow the individual to do what they do. Most such roles arise in the day-to-day running of a service or projects, whether formally or more informally; and most of the relationships that a service can create - the central tools for engagement - will arise out of the nature of any particular role or roles.

Formal and more structured roles, such as keyworker, peer mentor, or user group representative can offer opportunities to engage, to try new things, to grow. But so can much more informal roles, such as feeding the cat. Out on the streets, people often do have informal roles, as members of a street community. It's important to recognise and to build on such strengths.

Other roles in a service may be more 'outward-facing', in improving contacts and communications with other agencies. These kinds of roles can make a huge difference to smoothing the pathways to other supports for service users into and within the service, and in moving on. Many services now designate a 'PIE lead', as a person able to interpret and support the services development as a PIE, and PIE leads from different services and agencies can confer on working together better.

Responsiveness

Finally we wanted to have something about how the unwritten rules can shape the culture of an organisation, the rather more intangible aspects of the 'feel' or the culture of the organisation, as it affects the users.

We have called this the 'responsiveness' - how flexible or variable the service can be and, for example, how 'personalised'. By its nature it is hard to give examples of such flexibility; but we can say that the greater the focus on person-centred work in a service, the more flexible it must be.

The level of delegation in the management structure of a service (and/or the flexibility in the contract by which it is funded) will have the most impact here; and where the funders and commissioners avoid micro-management in the contracting process, and are willing to let the services they fund evolve and be more experimental, we tend to see services more responsive to changing needs.

But perhaps the most effective way to hear about the overall responsiveness is through service users' feedback, user consultations, co-production - or even fully user-led services.

WORKING WITH SPECIFIC ISSUES OR FOCUS

For the moment at least, the PIEs 2.0 framework remains our best attempt to sum up all the essential features that describe the work of a PIE, in quite generalisable terms (and therefore a somewhat abstract language). But before we move on from this outline of the overall framework, there is one last point to add.

In any general framework it is important to allow some flexibility, to ensure that there is all the responsiveness and focus that any service or network may need. The advantages of a holistic framework are clear; but sometimes it may be hard to locate a complex, multi-faceted response clearly and usefully within the five themes or the fifteen elements here.

More recently we have been exploring the possibility of adding in an extra element, for 'any other considerations' - any issue that is more specific to a particular service, or a particular way of working, or to any immediate concerns that need a particularly clear focus and coherence at any one time.

This can be quite useful, and with some care this is in fact fairly easy to do. But it does need some care when used in a network of services that wish to share their experiences, so we will look at some of the issues to consider in the context of sharing and pooling assessments and plans using the Pizazz and the PIE Abacus, in that chapter later.

In any case, in order to get the most of this new feature without losing the benefits of a single, coherent, shared framework, it is something that we would suggest is best when co-ordinated by a single individual in each agency or network. Experience in any case suggests that the work of translation from the general framework to the specifics of each service is most effective when there is at least one individual who is fairly familiar with the framework, and the underlying spirit; and fairly confident with the process.

We will call such a person the 'PIE lead' in any agency or network; and in the next chapter we'll start by taking a look at some general advice for such PIE leads, and any others who are concerned with how best to introduce this new way of seeing the work, whether to any one service, or throughout any agency or network.

Here we will also look closer at many of the other questions that will often arise in using the PIEs framework - at least, those that we find are most commonly asked - to equip you with some of the answers.

Then finally we'll cover the Pizazz - the self-assessment and service audit process that we have since developed, to help services to ask yourselves where you are, and where you want to be, in working in this way. This is where we will offer some more detailed advice on the best way to include 'any other considerations'.

CHAPTER SIX

INTRODUCING THE PIES APPROACH

Some general advice on developing as a PIE

Whether entirely new to the PIEs approach or re-visiting the issue and the PIElink website after some time away, there is some fairly sound general advice to share, gathered from ten years (and counting) of experience, on how to help your staff to get the most out of what the PIE approach and the PIES 2.0 framework is trying to do.

So we begin with some general points that are really as much to do with the spirit of the approach, building on the story of the PIEs origins with which we began. Here we have emphasised that the PIEs framework is not a list of things to do, but a way of looking at your work, that helps you see it all in a new light. What you then do, in your particular situation and services, is up to you.

This means that there is no one right way to 'be' a PIE; and likewise, there is no right way to develop as one, and to introduce the PIE approach in your services. Unless you are designing an entirely new service from scratch, developing an existing service will depend on two things: where you are coming from, and where you wish to go. Both will be unique to you. These ideas are therefore just the beginning of a discussion you will need to have, talking it over with operational staff.

We do strongly advise, though, that you aim to take this at the natural pace of your own services' development, as far as you can. A PIE approach is something that by its nature emerges from the discussions within a service. It can be embedded throughout an agency, and works best when it is. But it is not something that can be imposed from above, by senior management, however well intentioned; or from outside, by funders, however keen. It works 'from the ground up'.

The formative appraisal approach in practice

One thing we can say with confidence is that developing as a PIE is not a linear process, one with a start and a finish. It doesn't have an end point. The process is circular; and it gradually becomes part and parcel of your everyday working.

We have stressed that the PIE approach is 'holistic' - it aims to look at your services 'in the round'. But that also means that it is a multi-faceted approach; and you will be able to go further and faster in some areas than in others. (We will look into this more later, under 'Can a service be a little bit PIE'd?'). So a change in any part of the whole will mean changes for the whole.

In any case, human needs are not static. Needs change - and so do opportunities. A small change in the way some other services in your area work can create new openings or erect new barriers to working together. Changes in national policy and funding can have a quite immediate impact on gaps 'on the ground'. Other changes may have more of a slow burn effect, with their full consequences taking years to unfold.

Start with what matters most just now

So you can start anywhere; and the obvious place to start is with whatever matters most to your services at any one point in time. For example, a pressing issue in one agency or area might be staff welfare (Training and Support); or developing reflective practice (towards a Learning and Enquiry mode).

Another example might be focussing on particular issues, such as elastic tolerance and/or working with substance abuse (in the Three Rs); or being gender or ethnicity sensitive (with a more focused 'psychological/emotional awareness' applied to these issues); or improving pathways and partnership work with other agencies (opening and creating these new spaces of opportunity).

We suspect though that you will soon find that whatever particular issues you choose to focus on, the relevance of all the other themes then becomes apparent, as you begin to work through the practical implications of any one focus on your work in other areas. This is almost the hallmark of a holistic approach - that everything is connected.

Service-led assessment

Wherever you may feel you are, though, a self-assessment approach can be a helpful way to begin, taking a careful look at the service now, and then going on to assess current strengths and constraints for yourself, and forming an action plan.

This is in fact the approach we use with 'the Pizazz', whether on paper or using the software, so we will explore that in more detail in the next chapter. In fact, a lot of the general advice here on developing as a PIE is woven into the Pizazz so thoroughly that you may actually find this as a good a place to start as any. It gets you into it fast.

It does seem to help, to get into the detail - to make it all more tangible, practical and immediate. So we do encourage team self-assessment of services, because that's where you can make the most immediate changes together.

But to make sense of the Pizazz, your staff still need a general sense of what the PIE is about; and at least some familiarity with the frameworks we have developed to help to spell it out in practice, PIEs One and PIEs 2.0. So here, we have put those first in the book - from chapters Three to Five; and now, let's look closer at the relative strengths of each.

Comparing the two versions, PIEs One and PIEs 2.0

As an account that needs only five or six main concepts, the relative simplicity of PIEs One has some definite strengths. It is more clearly focussed on the inner workings of services. It goes into less detail on how to operationalise these issues than the later version; and this leaves those using it quite free to find in it whatever they need, and whatever best suits their own imagination for their services. In consequence, many services do find it useful and sufficient to their needs, at least initially.

Many of the reports and studies written before PIEs 2.0 was published have of course only used the original, 'classic' version, without mentioning any newer account; and this does sometimes add to the confusion. But it is perhaps the inevitable price to pay for a fast evolving world.

In each case, though, rather than giving a 'paint it by numbers' guide to 'how to be a PIE', both the PIEs formulations aim instead to give broad guidelines only. In each case, how you might now interpret and use these in your own services is up to you.

You may note that PIEs 2.0 separates out the single theme of 'Training and Support' into its two constituent parts. That's partly because PIEs 2.0 goes into more detail on all the big themes; but partly also because in practical application, training and support are often treated as separate elements, often with separate budgets. In large organisations they may even have separate departments for each. Therefore when getting into the operational detail of what may need to change, it can be valuable to separate them out.

Where the two most differ however is how they see 'managing relationships' or 'making relationships central'. Even the central significance of working with and through relationships, which we now see as pivotal, really emerged only in the course of the discussions that followed our first accounts of what we saw. (In this, though, the PIEs development was not alone; in various areas we now see relationship-focussed working being recognised as more useful - especially for some users, and for complex needs - than more single-minded task-focused work).

In PIEs One, making relationships central is a distinct issue, on a level with the other themes to be explored. In PIEs 2.0, by contrast, relationships are seen as central to absolutely everything, and this means they show in every area. The up-dated framework focuses instead on the more specific operational manifestations, such as in the emphasis on empathy and a broader psychological awareness, then the adoption of particular techniques, and finally of any specific 'psychological model', where that is clearly appropriate to the needs of the users of any particular service.

But there are gains and losses in this change. Many services do report that the 'centrality of relationships' concept has the most traction in helping staff think about what is most important in their work. It is still popular as a key issue. It is more inspirational than operational; but that is no bad thing.

As a general guide, PIEs One may be most useful and relevant where a staff team is new to the idea, and needs a fairly concise introduction; where it is important to start with the suggestion that it is the relationships that you can form that will be the key agents of change; and/or where much of a service's work takes place within a specific site or building.

Note that the Pizazz, when we come to describe it in more detail, uses the wider PIEs 2.0 framework. For those that do want to keep the centrality of relationships from that original wording, the best advice we have currently is to include this, and 'write it in' as a bespoke theme, alongside the other key themes, as we now can with 'Any other considerations'.

Then in team discussions on what actually happens in practice, the service's actual operational practice in making relationships central can be spelled out and explored. In the chapter on the Pizazz, we'll go into this in a little more detail.

Aiming for a still more versatile specification

One of the bolder claims in the PIEs approach, in both frameworks, is that there may be a single fairly coherent way of thinking and acting that underlies all the examples that we explored here. It was there, but it just hadn't been spelled out quite like this before.

The intention of PIEs 2.0, as the expanded PIEs framework, was not just to sum up what works within each specific service. It was to create a summary of ideas and practice that can create a common language for all services working with people with complex needs to share the same understanding of how they can make progress; and how they might then work more closely together.

This new framework then needed to be comprehensive, and more 'cross-platform', to work in many different settings and sectors. It needed to be inclusive, working for all levels of development and appreciative of all efforts, from whatever baseline. It needed to be scalable, to work with any size of service, network or organisation.

A single framework

This is a huge ambition; and it can only be realised if the language is fairly non-specific, and if services are then able to adapt and 'customise' this broad, generalised language to suit their particular work. What we aim for here is the underlying issues that most, if not all, these services have in common. The corresponding page with this heading on the PIElink spells out some of the requirements for such a language; and goes on to look more closely at the advantages and disadvantages in aiming to capture all this in a single framework for all 'complex needs' work.

You may note that this page uses the image of the Rosetta stone, the carved stone text whose discovery and eventual translation first made it possible to find the common meaning in long-forgotten ancient languages and cultures. The PIEs 2.0 framework, we meant to suggest, by being as broad and as comprehensive as possible, may now make it possible to translate between the concerns and terminology of other services for people with their complex needs.

In many parts of the UK, as in many other countries, a growing understanding and recognition of trauma via Trauma Informed Care is already helping to provide a shared awareness between services of the nature of the underlying problems that challenge services. The PIE approach, with its more detailed exploration of particular services' responses via the PIEs 2.0 framework, may now be able to complement and extend this awareness.

With a shared vocabulary for the more operational and more systemic issues, we may be able to address the working practices between services that can enhance or inhibit better collaboration between services, and help us arrive at more constructive ways to manage people's complex needs together.

CHAPTER SEVEN

GOOD QUESTIONS

Going a little deeper

This book is intended as an extended beginners' guide to PIEs. But even beginners will sometimes want to ask awkward questions. In fact, it is probably the beginners who are more likely to; and that's a very good thing.

So this chapter aims to be particularly relevant to all those who may now be tasked with leading on the introduction of the PIE approach in particular services or a network. We call this person the 'PIE lead'.

It is because of the need for flexibility that we have stressed the underlying spirit of the PIE approach early in the book; and the need to interpret the core themes and the practice elements into the terms and context of your own work. But it is the PIE lead, along with any more local PIE champion, that most needs the confidence to take these concepts and examples and use or apply them as you need, in context.

For these and any others ready to explore in a little more depth what the PIEs approach has for you, with the website and this small book working in tandem, we can now begin to dig a little deeper. In this chapter we will look at some of the most common concerns and objections that have been expressed to the whole approach, that you may encounter. There is something in most of them.

Where did it all come from?

Earlier we gave a fairly brief account of the evolution of these ideas in practice, up to the development of the PIEs 2.0 formulation and the reasons for it, meaning to stress the value of action learning, and the roots of the PIE in development in dialogue. This suggested some of the context in which first the actual practice and then the idea of PIEs had developed.

It is time now to tease out a little more of the history and the context in which these new ways of working and this new thinking came about. Though some of this is perhaps mainly of interest to historians of mental health and social policy, it may be helpful for PIE leads to know a little more of the story of how this approach came about.

Knowing the history helps, for example, to understand why there came to be various different versions of the PIE framework, either slightly or quite significantly different, as the ideas and the practice co-evolved over some ten years and more, because this can sometimes cause some confusion.

As it was described in the opening presentations to the (UK) first national conference on research and evidence in PIEs (in 2017), it was a combination of circumstances, influences and opportunities from social policy, social psychiatry and psychology that gave rise to the PIEs approach; and there was a string of happy accidents that brought all these together.

Social psychiatry was entering the era of community mental health, and through an initiative from the Royal College of Psychiatrists, was looking for a language to describe positive public health as seen in ordinary, non-clinical settings. Meanwhile, in the growing field of public health there was a wider developing understanding of the nature and prevalence of trauma, and the long term impact of adverse childhood experiences (ACEs).

Several social inclusion policy initiatives at the turn of the century were building on and re-enforcing progressive ('enlightened') practice developing in work with the marginalised and stigmatised. One these in particular, the Supporting People programme, helped to map out a fairly extensive and comprehensive overview of the range of ways that some services 'at the chalkface' were developing.

The paper in a mental health journal that had first actually suggested the term 'a psychologically informed environment' saw it simply as a handy description of the increasing sophistication being found in the responses of some of these services - but especially in homelessness resettlement

A UK government document of guidance for homelessness services published that same year (2010) then adopted the term, and was a little more explicit. It did attempt to describe what a PIE might looked like in practice, and it cited a dozen or so case studies as examples of effective and creative work. But the main thrust of that document was to stress the importance of recognising the role of understanding 'complex trauma', and of finding effective ways to respond.

That first guidance document was quickly followed by a second, 'operational' guidance (2012). This was more explicit in some areas, for example in suggesting the importance of 'having a psychological model'. But it was careful not to recommend any one particular model, instead stressing the importance of understanding the particular 'user' and their particular needs.

Subsequent accounts have tended to be still more open to new ideas and methods, drawing insights from as wide a range as occupational therapy, organisational psychology, business studies, sociology and anthropology, liberation theology and contemporary neuroscience.

There is a more detailed summary on one page on the PIElink; and for historians, from that page there are further links to still more detailed accounts of the discussions at each stage. These include more discussion on the limitations and the reasons for revising the PIEs One formulation, and the work on expanding its scope with what later became PIEs 2.0.

It is also worth reading the accounts on the PIElink of the parallel development of various comparable initiatives over this time, such as Housing First, Trauma-Informed Care, and Pretreatment, to help understand better the connections.

Finally, for those keen to see how things are continuing to develop, you might at some point want to get really up to date with where we are going in the future. It is possible for example that we may yet see a new and still broader version of the PIEs framework one day - we've called it 'PIEs 3'. This is not likely soon; but if you are interested in wider systems and system change, do see the discussion on where we are currently, on the page called '*Systems and system change?*'.

What 'psychology' makes for a PIE?

The United Kingdom is unusual in putting psychologists in the 'thought leadership' and research role in homelessness. In most modern societies, homelessness is seen as an issue for social services, and social work. It is only the particular history of social policy in the UK, and the exceptional growth of what became known as 'housing related support' that explains this difference, rather than any specific methods or skillsets.

On the whole, it usually is useful to have psychology input, though it perhaps depends on the psychologist. But as to whether it is actually necessary to have a psychologist on the team 'to do the informing', then the answer is clearly: it's *not*. We have argued consistently that the core 'psychology' needed is not a specialism, but is ordinary human empathy - and without that, no other more theoretical or technical skills will be able to take effect.

Nevertheless, what kinds of 'psychology' in the more technical sense might we then want, to 'inform' a psychologically informed environment? There are, as you might expect, a number of pages on the website discussing the contribution of various schools of psychology, and the techniques and approaches that stem from each. In one of these pages in the Resources Hub we also include just a small selection of 'snippets' - some less obvious, some almost quirky, un-categorizable but still very useful insights. Most of these do not belong to any particular school of thought.

But if there is to be a general rule, in the spirit of the PIE approach, it is that as and when any agency, or any particular service, decides to adopt any particular psychological model to provide coherence to its work, the important thing is that it is for a clear reason, and open to question.

What is 'an environment'?

Despite the fact that this is a key term here, it is almost impossible to define 'an environment', let alone to make a list of them. That's because in one sense, 'the environment' simply means whatever is all around whatever it is that you are primarily interested in.

In nature, there is the one big thing that we call the earth, as an environment. Within that, each particular environment is unique. Nevertheless some - such as a dessert, a sea shore, an inner city - have enough in common with each other that we can identify the key features of each type; and find the terminology to describe them and understand them.

That's really all we are doing, with the PIEs 2 framework - finding a language to help to identify the key features some have in common. Even so, as you know by now, you will have to adapt and adjust the terms for each particular setting.

What is more, there are environments within environments. Like a rock pool on a sea shore in the winter in the northern hemisphere, every environment is nested inside another, wider environment. Similarly in the case of complex needs services, every service is nested inside some agency, that provides it.

Each agency will also be one among many operating in the same area. Each network will be managed by some kind of planning and co-ordinating body, usually the local authority. Each local authority then works within the framework of legislation and funding of the higher authority, usually the government. Even the government works within an environment of policies and values, a mindset that it shares with the local population.

The PIEs 2.0 framework attempted to find a common language that all these environments can use. It seems to be reasonably successful; but it's a lot to try to do, and a lot will depend on how far you can interpret it all usefully, in the context of your own work.

Meanwhile, all environments are where they are not just in space, but in time. Like a rock pool on a sea shore in the winter in the northern hemisphere in an era of global warming, environments will change. That's why working as a PIE means constantly asking: so where are we now?

This is why we say that every environment is unique; and as a PIE, you have to explore yours - and that of your service users - for yourself. You can use the language and the tools that we have developed here; but the way you use them has to be your own.

That's also one of the reasons it's simply not possible to evaluate the benefits - or measure the 'improved outcomes' - from working 'as a PIE'. What you may get from it depends entirely on what you do with it. We will come back to the issue of evaluation later.

Can a service be 'a little bit PIE'd'?

The PIE 2.0 framework that we have developed to attempt to capture the underlying essentials has its five main 'themes', and within each of these main themes, there are between two and four more specific practice elements, to focus on the more practical elements, which we looked at in more depth in a previous chapter (for those of you that may have skipped to here....)

The PIE approach then aims to present a holistic model for services. That is, it suggests we want to see services as a whole, and consciously attempt to get the benefits of having all the elements working together, as a whole. But does everybody have to do all the things in this framework, in order to 'qualify' as a PIE - to be seen as part of the 'PIEs family'?

Surely not. There have been some really good services that used and developed only some part of the full PIE framework, with great success; in the case studies pages we have attempted to pick out a few. There are many in the same spirit that used different language to describe their efforts. After all, before 2010 we didn't even have the phrase, let alone the more specific description. Yet it's from them that we have learned.

We'd like to think that behind any specific action lies the rest of the thinking, however under-stated; or at least, the attitude, informing the specific activity. But we can still ask how relevant some parts of the framework are to some services. The five broad themes - the 'Big Five' - may well have some application just about everywhere, but there are clearly some more specific practice elements that won't apply to all services - or at least, will mean something fairly different, and need a lot of interpreting in context.

'Pick and Mix' with the PIEs 2.0 framework

Let's take a couple of examples. Take 'using psychological models'. Some services - especially treatment services - may well want to work to a quite specific model. Such intensive work benefits from the clarity and consistency in teamwork that a specific model can offer. But many, perhaps the majority of services will not, needing the flexibility to respond to any individual or situation on their own terms.

Or take 'encouraging evidence-generating practice'. Relatively few services are in a position to contribute to the kinds of studies that make for publishable findings of the kind that can appear in an academic journal, to contribute to the evidence base for PIEs, or for any other aspects of this work. It is not an expectation for all PIEs, just an option for a few.

Then, take working with 'the built environment': Firstly, some services, such as street outreach, do not have a building of their own, to adapt or 'pay attention to'. The skills in working in someone else's environment will be different, although they may be comparable, and there is some overlap.

Likewise, this can work in the converse direction. There may be some issues that a particular services wants to focus particularly closely on - perhaps just for a period, or perhaps because that is the specialism of the service, and it deserves greater focus. For this, the 'Any other considerations' advice in the chapter on using Pizazz and the PIE Abacus has some more detailed guidance on how to include and manage any such additional focus.

Welcoming challenges

But first, let's look at some challenges to this approach. The whole approach of a psychologically informed environment, and the adoption of any 'psychological model' and all the rest, comes with a clear recognition that challenge is good. Any real embedding of ideas in a service only comes when staff - and service users - are able to question how the service runs, and be involved in making changes.

It is true that there are some questions that you can only properly answer for yourselves, in the context of your own particular service or services. But there are some challenges that we have often encountered to the PIE approach itself. We should positively welcome such questions and challenges.

It's hard - and not necessarily even helpful - to categorise opinions. But it may be safe enough to say that there are a few schools of scepticism about the value of PIEs, with some justification; and at least one outright dismissal, without any; but that is easily corrected.

"It's just another fad - more buzz words....."

Sadly this is often true. It is all too possible to decide to call a service a PIE, but with only lip service, and little real understanding. Typically this is done quite opportunistically, just because commissioners may have stipulated - quite unhelpfully - that the services they fund should 'be' a PIE.

At worst, a cluster of quite superficial 'add-ons' may be introduced, as a tick box exercise. Or they may be imposed from outside the team or service, at the behest of 'the Top Brass', bent on 'implementing the PIE'. The central value and process of self-assessment and self-development is then sidelined, and may be entirely missed.

It is also common to find services, when they finally get to hear what this is really about, saying: 'Well, this is nothing new. Now we realise we were doing some of this all along'. It is important to value those voices that say: 'This is nothing new'. The PIE framework is just a way to see things more clearly; and then go on to ask: `Okay; so now what might you do?'

"It's too much to ask. We don't have time for this"

This is another valid challenge. The enthusiasm for PIEs has ramped up expectations as to what services will do, without necessarily any real change in the resources, and especially in the wages of staff.

The only real answer we have to this challenge is that, done properly, the PIE seems to be a great way to appreciate, to motivate, and to keep, your staff. If it's not as good as paying them well, it may be the least you can do. But the evidence - such as it is - does suggest that introducing some PIEs practice may also reduce challenging behaviour amongst service users. It can make your work easier.

Plus, as we noted earlier, some of the earliest published reports on the use of the Pizazz self-assessment process to develop services was that it seemed to bring benefits for staff morale. It seems that being listened to, and given some scope for leading on developments in services, was actually good for staff morale. This shouldn't be a surprise.

"Where is the data, so that we can be sure this is effective" and/or "It's just not evidence-based"

It is largely true that the PIE approach is not evidence-based, although only in a rather narrow sense of the word 'evidence'. The PIE approach arose out of some fifty years of experimentation in social psychiatry, and almost as a long a time - certainly thirty years - in homelessness work.

But this is not laboratory research, consistent and replicable, with random controlled trials and clear quantifiable results. This world is not like that. The key evidence is what we learn from experience. To compare the PIE approach with, for example, CBT, or Valium, is simply to misunderstand the nature of the PIE as a framework.

The PIE approach and the specific framework(s) are not a new set of things to do, which must be evaluated, individually or collectively. It is a new way to see what you DO do, in order to help you to think about what you could do. Like any tool, it's only as effective as the way it's used. You would not ask a carpenter to show the research on the effectiveness of chisel. It's simply the wrong question to ask.

Research and evaluation is always a tricky area for any kind of holistic and flexible services. In fact, the presentation that launched the working party from which the PIEs 2.0 framework grew eventually had made this - the need for a framework that is at least more 'research-ready' - one of the key reasons for the development of the up-dated framework.

Granted the sheer complexity of the issues, plus the extent to which research and evaluation in PIEs has to question many of the 'standard paradigms' of research and evaluation, with their roots in often unhelpful policy, there are now multiple PIElink pages on research and evaluation.

This is clearly an area more for the specialists - researchers and those business managers needing answers to questions from funders on the evidence of 'effectiveness' - than for the ordinary 'beginner'. To explore all this in the level of detail that it deserves is not relevant to everyone; so we can save any further discussion for the 'Digging Deeper' areas of the website itself.

Working with other models (such as TIC, HF etc)

Sometimes people who are new to the PIEs approach will ask: what then is the relationship between PIEs and Trauma-Informed Care (TIC) or Housing First (HF), or the strengths model, or some other? How do they fit together? Isn't there a lot of overlap? Do we have to choose which one to use?

Fortunately this one of the easiest questions of all to answer. This is simply a misunderstanding. The PIE approach is not an alternative model to many others; it is a way of looking at ALL services, to see what we need to do in practice, to implement whatever chosen approach it may be. As we see it, TIC and HF, for example, are both working examples of psychologically informed environments in practice.

In TIC it is specifically the psychology (and neuroscience) of trauma that is adopted as the 'psychological model'. From this central concept come all questions over the practical implications for training and support of staff; the way the agency or service runs, with its day-to-day rules, roles and procedures, the use of space and its subtle ('social') messages, and the pathways into and through the service, and so on.

Trauma-informed care in fact has some very similar 'higher order' big themes; and this is no surprise, as they both stem largely from the same roots, in combining emerging practice in services with the emerging theory - in this case specifically research into trauma.

Where they differ is simply in the greater clarity of PIEs 2.0 in the operational expression of the 'practice elements'. This is why many TIC services in the UK are now adopting the PIEs framework (and the Pizazz) as an effective way to implement and embed TIC in their services.

When Housing First really works, it seems, it is because these services must work with all the issues that may arise in homelessness and complex needs. The issues that are too flexible and contextual to be included in the research and policy for the tighter specification of the Housing First model are precisely those we try to explore, via the PIEs framework.

In Housing First it is the Three Rs that take centre stage; the 'non-negotiable' principles of HF create the defining rules of the approach. The specification that housing comes first is the fundamental rule; it follows from this that HF service users must have a full standard tenancy agreement, and from that, that tenants' acceptance of any support must be voluntary. Technically the 'psychological model' here is secondary; although TIC is often recommended and the strengths model is at the very least implicit, they are not specified, expected or required as part of the model.

It may seem a little paradoxical to say that there is a rule that there shall be no further rules over people's behaviour, over and beyond the ordinary terms of a tenancy. But that is still the foundational rule for all services that want to be in the HF camp. All other techniques and roles then follow from that central rule, and they have to be devised by the service providers with all the creativity that they can manage, customised to particular circumstances.

It is true that the PIE framework can be used in hostels (or 'shelters') - just the kind of transient accommodation that is often seen as unnecessary and even negative by some of the more assertively single-minded proponents of Housing First. But to suggest that we don't need temporary accommodation, so we don't need PIEs is simply a misunderstanding . (It's what philosophers have called a 'category error').

Nesting other models within the PIEs framework

So as we see it TIC and HF are fully compatible with being PIEs. They are both comfortably nested within the broader framework that PIE offers. But we can go a little further. It does seem that when people are struggling to work out the best way in practice to implement TIC or HF in their service and in their particular context, to use that creativity that they need to meet the principles, the PIEs framework helps to identify more concrete and specific next steps.

Certainly that is the message that we have been getting from many services that have wanted to get the best of both. The PIE framework takes you on further, to look at the areas where the chosen model had either stopped short (in HF), or been too general and imprecise to be immediately translated into all the practical implications (in TIC). The Pizazz in particular is designed to help services tease out for themselves where they can make changes.

We have begun, and hopefully will continue, exploring how best to use the PIE approach in some of the forums and specifically in one of the PIElink's Special Interest Groups. It may even prove that some explicit guidance or examples of PIEs in HF, and HF in PIEs, might be helpful.

A number of other similar questions can be resolved in the same way: where do we find the strengths model, or ecotherapy (a.k.a 'greencare'), pre-treatment, appreciative enquiry, human learning systems? The strengths model, for example, is generally highly commended in HF services - as is TIC. But as a model it is entirely compatible with TIC, and is usually incorporated into most versions of TIC in practice. You don't have to choose between one or the other.

The strengths model is actually derived from a humanistic psychology school known as positive psychology (that is, it looks for and learns from the positives in human behaviour rather than always focussing on the deficits). In PIEs terms, therefore, it provides an approach to psychological awareness that has a lot to offer. The PIEs framework then just gives you a useful and manageable structure to work with, to look at the service as a whole to see how far it reflects that model as a way of thinking about people – to operationalise it.

The same can be said of many other particular 'approaches and techniques', such eco-therapy, animal-assisted therapy, activity-based projects such as employment or skills training workshops or community gardens; they may all find in the PIEs 2.0 framework a useful way to explore their embedding in the service as a whole.

Similarly with more system-focussed approaches to communications, such as Open Dialogue, person-centred research, 'Enabling Help' or 'Human Learning Systems'. These are all located comfortably within the Learning and Enquiry theme, with implications to tease out then to the other practicalities of putting this thinking into practice. In fact, this may yet prove to be the most radical part of the PIE approach - the scope to include whole systems in the analysis of what works and what hinders.

Note that when thinking to adopt a specific model in a service it may then be helpful, at least initially, to write in a bespoke field for this in your assessment, to integrate and embed this through the service. This will be another case for using the 'Any other considerations' option, and we will look into the potential for this in the next section, on using Pizazz and the PIE Abacus.

Other questions

Most questions, including the trickiest, do not come in the form of outright challenges, but rather arise in the course of attempts to explore how the PIEs approach works in any particular context.

Over the past ten years, over the course of hundreds of presentations and conversations on-line, the PIElink has amassed many recordings of such explorations of topics and questions, between them covering most aspects of the development of PIEs, translating theory into practice, and vice versa.

The on-line forums that ran over the course of the COVID pandemic era of 2021 were recorded, to be shared later with participants; and where appropriate (and only with consent) we have some edited extracts. Some interviews were conducted with the express intention of sharing the contents with particular teams.

As with the case studies of particular practice or contexts, it is often almost impossible to categorise many of these free-flowing discussions. But in some cases where there was a particular topic to discuss, we do have recordings that we can now share, and these are integrated into the pages on the PIElink relating to the topic in question.

'Useful questions'

Finally, this openness to challenge extends to questioning what 'being a PIE' really means, for any service; and even - as we have just seen - how suitable it really is, as a model to use.

When we come on to exploring the Pizazz, in the next chapter, you will see that the Pizazz Facilitator's Handbook, '*Useful questions*', is quite explicit that challenge and disagreement as to what the PIE approach really means in any one context is to be welcomed. It is part of the 'culture of enquiry', rather than expecting a culture of adherence. In this way, the underlying thinking (and 'reflective practice') needed for a PIE can be kept live and relevant.

Whether or not you may be using the Pizazz process - on paper or on screen - to take a look at your services 'through the PIE lens', you will find some useful questions to ask yourself in the '*Useful questions*' handbook, which you will find in the members' library. (Remember though that you will need to register, to access a copy.)

CHAPTER EIGHT

PIZAZZ AND THE PIE ABACUS

Taking the next steps

Up to this point we have only mentioned the Pizazz - the PIEs Self-Assessment and Service Specification process - in passing. But we have mentioned it with increasing frequency, because the further you get into the PIEs idea, the more useful the Pizazz starts to be.

The Pizazz process was originally devised as a means for those further advanced in their development as PIEs, now wanting to assess their progress against a measure of success. But the Pizazz is more than just an assessment tool. It is a process for identifying necessary and possible adjustments and change in some detail. It is a formative assessment process; and so it becomes a change management tool, with the changes coming 'from the ground up'.

That principle of self-assessment is important. We suggest that self-assessment will tend to be more engaging, and probably more honest, than assessment by any external accreditation body. Senior management and funders can endorse and can encourage 'bottom up' development as PIEs; but they cannot impose it without risking undermining the whole exercise.

We also find that self-assessment can explore the quality of a service's work in ways that any quantitative evaluation using standardised 'outcomes' cannot do. It can reach into the tiny operational details - what we have identified in the Three Rs - that make any agency policy work, or not work, in a specific context.

But it is not just that. The Pizazz is not just a way to embed the PIEs approach in any single agency. There is potential here for wider and more systemic change, looking outside the boundaries of an agency making its assessment and its own adjustments. The potential here is quite exciting, and potentially quite radical; but best seen in the software version, the PIE Abacus.

Meanwhile we are now hearing that many services have found it particularly useful in introducing the PIE approach in their services. With its emphasis on self-assessment and on service-led development, it seems to be very effective as a way to make clear the encouraging spirit and the underlying intentions of the PIEs approach. It's a way to engage your staff in the process from the start, making the general themes and language of the framework immediately relevant and practical.

Although it is clear that the real development of PIEs best starts 'from the ground up', in many areas funders (and even governments) are starting to endorse the approach, and in any larger organisation, managers may be keen on seeing more of their services developing as PIEs. It is then important that all staff understand the process, in order to make it their own.

But it is also possible that you and your staff may one day be invited to take part in a local area or network Pizazz assessment, even when the whole idea is still quite new to you. We will go into it here therefore, because it may prove useful even for quite tentative beginners. When ready, simply go to the PIElink (www.pielink.net) and look for '*Pizazz and the PIE Abacus*'. You really cannot miss it.

THE PIZAZZ

What IS the Pizazz?

The Pizazz is a carefully designed, structured process of self-exploration for services, intended primarily for use in teams to assess to what extent the service already does work in a PIE way; and then to see where and how they might bring out more, working together.

Even where services had not initially seen their work in these terms, and may now see themselves as being barely at the starting line, a Pizazz assessment will often show that a service may be already quite advanced in one or another aspect of the work. The Pizazz then helps them to see and to round out their work, where it seems valuable to do.

Every PIE is different, of course; which means that every would-be PIE needs to explore its own way forward; and it takes discussion in a team to do this. But team discussions without a structure can be circular, and then become self-defeating. When we are looking at how to improve a service, especially one intended to meet more complex needs, a structured process - with some flexibility built in - can really help.

That flexibility is key. Like the PIEs framework itself, the Pizazz has to be as versatile and adaptable as the services it works for. Like the PIEs framework itself, it's not so much a new set of things that a service must do to 'measure up', but rather a way to see, and to think through, what works for you. In essence it is simply another tool that anyone can use.

Why is it called 'Pizazz'?

'Pizazz' is a show biz term that means dynamism, flair, sparkle, and creativity - and maybe a hint of courage to stand out, and do something bold. We chose this as the name for an assessment tool for PIE services because the kind of services we see, and would like to see more of, display all those same characteristics.

The intention here was to try to capture and sum up the spirit in these services, not to dampen it down. This is what motivates staff to go into this work; it's never to improve the quantified outcomes of the service; it's because the work is satisfying, feels meaningful, rewarding. It has a buzz. The key criterion for an assessment process that helps services along on their PIE journey is that it should recognise that buzz; and aim to enhance it.

We do sometimes claim that this name is an acronym, and that these initials spelled out 'the PIEs Self-Assessment and Service Specification' process. But in truth, we started with the word 'pizazz', because what we wanted to capture was the creativity, the sheer pizazz, that we find in some services. Most assessment approaches tend at best to ignore, or at worst to stifle, this crucial element. Not here.

How does it work?

The Pizazz process comes in two formats - the pen-and-paper version, published in 2018 and now in widespread use across the UK; and the software version, known as the PIE Abacus, which was released only in 2021 and therefore is still fairly new. We are still exploring the full potential. To explain the common core of the process, it is easier to start with the pen-and-paper version.

To use the pen-and-paper version of the Pizazz, you need only download the paperwork pack from the website (www.pielink.net). It is available for any registered member of the PIElink to download entirely for free; and its easy to find.

There are a few pages of general advice in the pack, but the core of the process is contained in just one document - the 'summary sheets' - and just five pages, one for each of the five stages of your assessment and planning. These are:

- your initial thoughts on where you are at;
- your reasons for thinking so;
- a discussion on what might help you move on, and what holds you back;
- an action plan for what you now mean to do;
- as a final stage, a plan to review later where you have gotten to.

The issues you will then look at, working through these five stages, are of course those of the PIEs 2.0 framework. So anyone who has read this book will already be well familiar with the central themes, and the whole process should echo much of the spirit of the first chapters of this book, and in particular the chapter before this, on welcoming questions.

If it is PIEs One that you have used until now, as the core themes of PIEs One are included within PIEs 2.0, you can simply focus on the issues this version uses. You can ignore the others, or use them only where it make sense to do so, and so gradually extend into the new framework.

Do look out for the Pizazz Facilitators' Handbook, sub-titled *'Useful questions'*. These 'useful' or typical questions are intended simply to indicate the areas that services may want to look at, in assessing how far their service is developing as a PIE. Any particular service must decide which questions are the most relevant and useful to them, at their particular stage of evolution; and that should get you started on finding further questions, to make the process your own.

Making it work for you

For a discussion in a single team you can simply print out the summary sheets. Then with your staff and whoever else you may invite sitting around a table, you can work through your views and experiences, your comments on each of the areas of the framework in whatever level of detail you think useful. You might start with each individual initially recording their individual views, and later pooling them as a team view.

Do not skip this last stage. It is the team discussion, the exchange of views and the shared vision of what needs to happen next, that is the real outcome. You may use the suggested 'levels' to guide and give yourself a score on each of the various themes or specific elements; but the role of the scoring is to clarify the range of views. It is not to evaluate your service objectively, measured against some external yardstick.

In a larger group, to encourage more liveliness and movement and to open up the space for a more expansive discussion, you might copy the text onto a flip chart, a screen or a blackboard. Then you can use Post It notes for people's comments; and write up the shared conclusions at the end of the discussion. We know of some teams that then hang the resulting document like a chart on the office wall, to remind them of the issues and the direction they mean to go in.

Some have found that it's best to take time out to tackle a discussion of the whole service, in an Away Day or similar. Failing that, one PIE expert trainer suggests taking one of the five themes at a time, as a ten minute slot in a regular weekly or even monthly staff meeting, and to work through it all over the course of several weeks or months.

It's important to take this at a pace that suits you, that doesn't feel like a burden. There is even a whole page on the PIElink that suggests how anyone might undertake a thoroughly slimmed down and quite informal version of the whole approach, in the space of 10 to 15 minutes. Called '*The coffee break Pizazz*', it aims to de-mystify the process, and make it all seem entirely natural.

Using the 'Any other considerations' option

We have promised at several points earlier a comment on how to create 'bespoke' fields for 'Any other considerations' in any network. This option allows services to 'add in' any further specific issues of their own - that is, to introduce new specific questions that are of interest to a particular service, but had not been generally or not sufficiently highlighted in the overall main framework of PIEs 2.0.

It's always best to use the PIEs framework as far as possible to identify the key features of any service's work, even if at times it might take some interpretation or imagination to see how these themes apply in any particular context. This provides the common ground between teams and services, and allows your learning and development to be shared with others. Nevertheless, where there are issues that are particular to one service or network, and important to bring out, this is where you might use the 'Any other considerations' option.

For example, one (hypothetical) agency wishes to undertake training for a range of local community groups involved in a particular project. For this, the term 'Staff training and support' does not quite cover the area they want to focus on. So they add a third area in Training and Support, calling it 'community training' and there they might devise criteria of success that are entirely their own.

Another agency wants to focus for a period on their support to women. This issue touches on all aspects of the PIEs framework, and specific actions in detail can (and should) be addressed under each relevant theme; but this does not allow the coherent overview they wish for. So they add a new main theme, using 'Any other considerations', giving it a new title to bring together in one place all aspects of support to women.

This option was not part of the Pizazz process when it was first published, using the original PIEs 2.0 framework. This is because the intention and ambition was to create a single framework that a wide range of services could all use, whether that might be within in a large agency, across a local network, for a research group, or anywhere where we might develop the purpose and practice of PIEs.

For this to work as a common sharing platform, it had seemed important that all users of the PIEs approach and therefore of the Pizazz should be encouraged to use the same central framework, and attempt to locate all their particular activities as examples in practice, so that we can then pool experiences.

This remains a concern for any who wish to share, pool and analyse this information between a number of services with consistency, sufficient to analyse and learn from the bigger picture. The potential value in this wider sharing becomes clearer when we look next at the potential in the software version of the Pizazz, the PIE Abacus.

There is a solution; but here it starts to get more technical than we need, for an introduction to PIEs; and besides, we are still exploring the uses and benefits of the software. So as this is still a relatively recent development, it seems better to refer readers at this point to the PIElink for practical advice as to how best to manage this to best effect. There we can go into more technical detail, for those who wish to try it; and there we can update the advice, as we explore examples.

Peer review: the final frontier?

Once you have completed your first round of assessment and planning, the Pizazz process is then cyclical; you can repeat it, or return to it, and you can take as long on it as feels useful, each time you come back to it. In the same way that to work as a PIE you do not need to be aiming to do absolutely everything in the PIEs 2.0 framework, so likewise to review what you are doing, and where you might want to make progress, you don't need to do everything at once. It's perfectly ok - and natural - to prioritise what you want to focus on.

Once any service's own assessment and planning is completed, you can also share and pool some of your conclusions with others in your locality, for example to look at what needs to improve in the way your services and others work together. It fact, we do particularly recommend this, for those that are ready for it. So useful is this that we have built it in as a final stage for a full assessment - 'peer review' – although it has to be understood that not many teams or services will necessarily be ready to get to that stage in their first run.

Self-assessment with peer review can be a valuable mechanism for the kind of 'horizontal accountability' that we suggested earlier was an advantage in the principle of self-assessment of services. An invitation to peer review can then be a first tentative and modest step towards establishing a more collaborative relationship with others. As an extension of the scope of local sector engagement, this may even be the beginnings of the networking for 'whole systems work', that we will explore later, on the full potential in the PIE Abacus software.

Who you might then choose as a peer reviewer, when ready, will depend on many factors; but it really should be an agency that you feel safe enough with to be honest; and if they then choose to invite you to look at their work too, so that it is a mutual review, then so much the better for your closer working.

But now it's time to go further still.

THE PIE ABACUS
A bold new step on our collective journey?

So far we have described the Pizazz as primarily a process for teams, and illustrated it with the pen-and-paper version, which was first published in 2018, and is now in widespread use in the UK. But a software version, known as the PIE Abacus, finally went on general release in the spring of 2021. This is therefore still relatively new, and we are still exploring the potential it offers.

The PIE Abacus works to the same essential five-stage process; and as software, the Abacus has a wealth of other functions built in – far too many, in fact, to explore them all in a basic introduction. But the principal value of the software form is that you can more easily share some or all of your assessment and conclusions with colleagues, whether that be other teams in a large organisation, or in a network, without any constraints of distance. This development may prove to be the next major stepping stone in the whole PIEs journey.

At this point, however, any further exploration of what the PIE Abacus - the Pizazz in software form - can do will focus on a more advanced exploration of any service's role within the larger structures in which it is situated – whether in a large agency, or a local network of services.

This is probably mainly of interest to those in more senior management or development roles, and in larger agencies of networks. Others reading this far can stop now, and skip to the next chapter. But for senior managers or PIE leads in larger agencies or networks – do read on.

The added value of a software version

Three years and more in development, and building on 20 years' experience with this same software and approach in education, the PIE Abacus has been comprehensively adapted for our purposes in complex needs service work, and piloted with a dozen agencies of varying sizes across the UK.

It was designed first and foremost to give larger agencies and networks an overview of progress in their roll out of PIEs. But we should also look over the potential in this software for 'whole systems' work, and for system change, that is only now emerging.

The PIE Abacus takes the all same terms and processes as the Pizazz-on-paper, five themes and five stages, and puts them online. Instead of working through printed pages, those using the software go from screen to screen on a computer. The PIE Abacus is entirely online, so all the data that is 'in-put' is held electronically on a central site. In internet language, it is 'cloud-based'.

This gives a little more flexibility than the paper version did over what you might want to include to support and enrich the 'evidence' to back up your teams' views. It allows for example for hyperlinks to be added, and for any kind of information to be included – reports, spreadsheets, videos and website or other links – and shared.

But this is only the beginnings of the potential in now having the Pizazz in software form. Let's consider the implications and the possibilities that this opens.

Roll out in larger agencies and networks

A large agency may have many services that it manages, perhaps spread across a large geographical area. A national agency may have even local offices and services in every region and every locality. This makes face-to-face meeting to discuss issues of common concern harder - and far more expensive. The advantage of software here is that the information can be shared electronically; and as it then can be treated in effect as data, it can be pooled and analysed to provide a broad overview of progress - and significant gaps - across the whole agency.

As software, you can sort and filter the data in any way you chose. You might want to analyse the pooled data for patterns in views across the agency as a whole, whether in specific local services (such as: 'All those in the northern region'), or in particular sectors (such as: 'All outreach services', or 'All youth services') or across the board (such as: 'All training and support' policies).

This makes the Abacus a useful tool for managing the roll out of the PIEs approach, as seen from the perspective of the staff in local services who are in-putting their views on their own services. This includes their analysis of what barriers to progress they are finding, and what action they themselves mean to take; and where this action might need support or new approaches from the agency itself, this collectively pooled information may be invaluable.

The potential here lies in providing a means to hear directly from the people 'at the sharp end' about where the gaps and barriers are, as they see them. It is to be expected that this will result in a chorus of familiar complaints. But they can also be asked their view on what opportunities there may be, that current services specifications may be holding back. Staff and users are being invited to give their evidence for what holds the services back, and - via their action plans - where in detail they might be able to suggest what they might do differently, given the willingness of others to co-operate.

Such information from those well informed to suggest both large and small changes in working practice can be invaluable. The potential in creating an alternative channel for their views is clearly something to be explored. But the momentum to then enact these changes, having been heard, is probably more valuable still.

This information might of course be gleaned simply by asking all the participating services to send in the summary copies of their pen-and-paper assessments, to be collated and analysed by staff at Head Office. Up to a point, in a smaller agency or network this may be quite workable, and quite sufficient to provide the overview that is wanted.

It is when an agency has more than a dozen or perhaps a couple of dozen services that the advantage of pooling opinions and plans electronically becomes more apparent. The saving in the work of admin staff is evident; but so is the capacity for clarity in seeing what works, and what needs to change; and in tracking progress later.

Yet this potential benefit in the pooling of information applies not just to a range of services managed by any one agency, but also to more dispersed networks of independent agencies with some common purpose, who may also now share and pool their views on what works, and what holds them back.

Systems, pathways and partnership working

This same potential advantage in treating frontline staff's opinions and plans as information that can be shared and pooled applies where there are many services in any one locality needing to work more effectively together, and to share views on what impedes their working better; and what might be changed.

At this point we start to glimpse the ways in which this software provides a new communication channel - a new kind of communication channel - between local funders and planners and all the service providers, their staff and their managers, and their service users.

There is also the option of inviting parallel and quite independent assessments and views from services users themselves. Service user consultation processes in the past have tended to rely on surveys or large meetings to elicit the views of services users. But not everyone fills in survey questionnaires, or feels comfortable speaking up in a public space.

The principal limitation here maybe around how much services are willing to share with others - particularly over any weaknesses or inhibitions, or in their own overall assessment. Trust is necessary for honesty. But staff and users alike are often quite keen to give their opinions on what needs to change in the system as a whole.

The software has flexibility built in to adjust the sharing permissions, so that these can be set so that only certain information, such as that relative to local collective problems, bottlenecks and suggestions on improved pathways, will be shared and pooled. It would be counterproductive if local funders were to demand full disclosure. In any case, participation can be voluntary.

A note on the language of co-production

One of the challenges for the future is the fact that the Pizazz process works with the PIEs framework; and as we saw in earlier chapters, the PIEs 2.0 framework, in order to be comprehensive, is largely couched in a language which can seem quite abstract. This was, we'd argued, the price we must pay for a framework that aims to be holistic, responsive and inclusive; and it may at least help to find common ground with other agencies and sectors.

But the PIEs language is still the language of services, rather than the language of any service's users; and this is true of both PIEs One and PIEs 2.0. If we are serious about co-production of services - that is, involving service users in the whole process of evaluating and developing services, on the principle of 'nothing about us without us' - then there is a challenge here to be tackled.

If services are self-assessing and progressing and using the Pizazz process, online or on paper, we need a translation of the language into the language of ordinary people. In fact this may well apply not just to services' users, but often for the staff too, many of whom may at first find the abstract language quite off-putting.

Fortunately, we do have a solution of sorts. As chapter Six suggests, experience shows that the most effective way to introduce and to conduct a Pizazz audit in any service is to identify one or more individuals - the PIE lead or a local PIE champion - who is relatively confident of what it means, and what it can mean in that particular context. They will be familiar and comfortable with the process; and they can then 'customise' the more abstract terminology to suit the particular circumstances, the client group, setting, or approach.

For service user involvement in a service's self-assessment and development planning, it may be that that same individual is the person best placed to facilitate the assessment of users, using their own understanding of the issues to translate the PIE concepts into the language of lived experience, just as they do with their own services staff.

Alternatively it might be as or more suitable to bring in an advocacy service. Where the intention is to gain a service users' perspective on the gaps and barriers that we find in the systems and pathways around the service, it might well be particularly appropriate for the assessment and the feedback it generates to be facilitated by a fully independent person.

Further development

There may yet be further development work to undertake in the future, to get the maximum benefit from the potential in the Pizazz, both the paper and the software versions. For example, as the PIE approach spreads into new areas, the PIElink itself can accommodate new developments, but there may come a point at which it is necessary to revisit the kind of illustrations of PIEs in practice used in the Facilitators Handbook.

The practice of Housing First continues to gain momentum, and there has been a growing number of registrations for PIElink membership from staff in housing management and tenancy sustainment roles, which suggests that there may be a demand for more examples of effective approaches and techniques in support and management in people's own homes.

At the present there is only one version of the Handbook, and it attempts to suggest examples of activities that indicate working as a PIE across the whole spectrum of services. This helps to broaden the perspective you may take; but it may be that at some point in the future it may be helpful to produce more specialised versions.

One day we might perhaps have versions that go into more detail with working examples suited for particular services or groups, such as, for example, outreach workers and/or Housing First staff, or those working with addiction or severe mental illness, learning difficulties, or ageing well.

Research

There is one further possibility in using the PIE Abacus to mention here. There is also potential in sharing information purely for research purposes, and the capacity in future to produce large datasets of qualitative information creates a new instrument and a methodological innovation for evidence-generating practice.

Research into systemic change may also require systemic change in the methods and criteria of research. That is, in effect, another example of a systemic change – though not, in this case, in the ways that services are run and managed, but in the ways that we learn from what works. This is probably an issue of interest mainly to the more academic research community; but we mention it here as another example of the many inventive uses of any new medium.

Nevertheless, in discussions with Head Office or local commissioners over funding, the point of sharing the evidence on how things are, what works and what needs to change, is practical and fairly immediate. Service providers are stakeholders in the need for good quality, meaningful evidence; the point is to inform those with the responsibility for the whole over the potential for change.

The PIE Abacus for development in dialogue

Clearly much of this continuing exploration will now happen within services, within agencies, and in local or more specialist networks. But there is also scope in communicating the messages of this community-based action learning to those in government and in other regulatory bodies whose wish it is to advance social practice, in the widest sense.

There is great scope to learn from each other, and to share what we learn; and at some point, this needs something broader - some degree of collective facilitation and co-ordination of feedback. The question then is: how far can the PIElink and its membership, as a community of practice, usefully accommodate and facilitate such large scale discussions and learning?

Since this is a question about the future, though, it is time to wrap up this account of 'the PIEs story so far'. The final chapter here is about what happens next, not just in and with your own services, but in the wider picture, and where the PIElink - 'the once and future PIElink' - may be able to continue to play a constructive role in the development of the PIEs approach.

CHAPTER NINE

THE FUTURE FOR PIES

Where to next?

This final chapter is almost the shortest in the whole book. That is because the real work of charting and chronicling the futures of PIEs will be found not here, but on the PIElink. The task of this conclusion is simply to suggest a few issues, and point towards where to look for new developments.

That said, it is worth repeating that most of the more exciting work and learning happens in the services themselves. We are, in the words of one of the PIElink videos, constantly try to keep up with emerging practice.

Nevertheless one of the few real benefits from the COVID pandemic era was the familiarity with live streaming that it brought to so many people; and we have found it is particularly well suited to informal conversations and practice share between people, with no limitations of distance to inhibit us.

During 2021, one of the great innovations within the world of PIEs was the experiments with twice weekly live and interactive 'forums', via Zoom (also Teams and a few other platforms). These were opportunities for PIElink members and others to join the conversation on any given topic, live and in real time.

More engaging than full-size webinars, these events helped to develop a stronger sense of a community of practice, and to take some issues further. It began to really feel like a PIElink community. Future forums from 2023 and beyond will be able to pick up the thread. Anyone can join these discussions, whether registered or not; but those who are registered will get an email notification of forthcoming talks.

In addition to these forums, there were the beginnings of specific sub-groups meeting more regularly, whether as mutual support groups, as Action Learning Sets, or as working parties ('Special Interest Groups') to develop ideas on any particular topics of immediate interest.

There were some areas that were developing fastest in the months leading up to the publication of this book, and the semi-retirement of the PIElink's original founder and editor, Robin Johnson. (Robin being the original author, chief theorist and steward of the PIEs idea over the first decade of its evolution; and the author of this introduction.)

In the course of this book we have already indicated some of the areas where there seems the most potential, and/or the most need to continue further exploration of the potential and range of the PIE approach, and the use of the Pizazz and PIE Abacus.

For a short list, we might suggest:

- Housing First - a new edition of the Handbook to focus on examples of helping to make other peoples's environments work for them - to feel like their own home.
- Extending the range of this approach outside the UK, including in Europe, the US and Canada, and Australia.
- 'Fresh directions' - exploring the relevance of the PIE approach in other sectors and in work outside of welfare and homelessness services.
- Using the PIE Abacus - continuing the development of the software to be adaptable to new purposes.
- Exploring the complexities and potential of research and evaluation with a holistic model.
- Finding a more service-user friendly language for PIEs.
- Using PIEs, the Pizazz and Abacus for whole systems work and system change.

On the website, via the *'Quick links'*, *'Hot Topics'* and other links on the *'START HERE'* page you will be able to track current progress on these issues. But there is one 'hot topic' in particular that stands out. That is: Using PIEs, the Pizazz and Abacus for whole systems work and system change.

Tackling whole systems

As we have argued, all environments exist within other, wider environments; and all consciously psychologically informed environments, however well intentioned, effective and even innovative, exist alongside and within other services and wider environments.

These are the local systems or 'eco-systems of services', which may support or may hinder their own efforts. In the third decade of the 21st century, many are now of the opinion that there is much in these systems that is dysfunctional, and calls for more widespread 'system change' are mounting.

Where then is the PIE approach going, to keep abreast of those services and local networks that are starting to tackle these wider challenges, let alone to assist and take a lead? Is there enough scope already, in the PIEs 2.0 practice elements of 'sector engagement' and in addressing local 'systems and pathways', to start tackling this wider environment in which services operate?

Is there sufficient breadth and flexibility already in PIEs 2 that we simply need to encourage and bring out, as a new vocabulary of 'customising'? Or will we need not just a new language but a whole new set of issues and themes in order to focus specifically on these eco-system issues, to expand the framework with the same breadth and clarity as PIEs 2.0 attempted to focus on the environment in and around their own services?

Will there one day need to be a new and still wider version of the PIEs framework, embedding upwards? Could there and should there be, in effect, a 'PIEs Three'?

This is a discussion which, at the time or writing, is just beginning. Certainly the potential in creating, via the PIE Abacus, a new kind of channel for local discussions on local needs and opportunities, is promising - but so far, only glimpsed.

As with everything that has marked the PIEs approach so far, it is only in use, in action learning and in development through dialogue, that we will see what this might yet open up. But it is one we hope to explore.

In conclusion

All conclusions are temporary. But some are more temporary than others.

We can anticipate that there will be fewer changes and additions to the essential PIEs framework, at least for a period. Nevertheless the PIE approach, and the specifics of the PIEs framework, continue to spread and to be adopted by new services, agencies and sectors.

How long the current shape of the site may last will depend on how fast things continue to develop. As and when there are new developments, though, the site itself will carry the news, via the '*Hot Topics*' link on the '*START HERE!*' page.

Until that day, this book stands as a record of where we had been able to take it to, in a little over ten years; and after this, dear reader, it is down to you. As indeed it always was.

POSTSCRIPT

In the conventions of book writing, even for a book that aims to be primarily factual, convention allows the author to make a more personal statement in the Postscript, as in the Preface, So here, in these final pages, I do get one last opportunity to be more myself.

This site, and all my work on PIEs, is predicated on the belief that we learn best, fastest and deepest, when we learn together; and that real change comes from that shared learning. This is an alternative, even an implied challenge, to the 'top down' or 'command and control' approach that has governed much of social welfare and similar services provision for much of my career, and beyond.

Of course, no-one need feel obliged to adopt this Big Idea, just to work in or run services, and to use the PIEs approach, the Pizazz and the PIE Abacus.

I've have tried hard, over several years, to present the whole thing as a box of tools to use only as it suits you, for whatever your purpose. I've hoped to be as helpful, even as modest, as I am ambitious. I've also tried hard to counter the view that the PIEs approach should, or even could, be imposed on services, staff and their service users.

So at the risk of repeating myself - yet again - let me end with one last reminder: don't take any of this as gospel. I may have been the person to first spot something going on, and to give it a name; later to elaborate, to think some things through, with the opportunity to attend or convene a string of discussions to share ideas and practice.

But this is not my work; it's yours. My words here are just my best attempt to sum up what I am hearing; and as I have said before: at heart there is only one true 'PIE principle', and that is that you must think for yourselves, decide together what to do, and own the changes. As I've said before: these words are our servants, not our masters.

Robin Johnson

About the author

Robin Johnson is a former therapeutic community social therapist, mental health social worker, author, editor, researcher, data and policy analyst, and now 'content provider'.

While working as UK national lead on mental health and housing for the National Social Inclusion Programme, his role included liaising closely with the Department of Health and the Department of Communities, and also with the Royal College of Psychiatrists on the 'Enabling Environments' programme.

During this time Robin suggested the term 'a psychologically informed environment' to describe the creative practice then emerging in homelessness services in the UK. In the years since then, he and his colleagues have refined these initial observations into a dynamic working framework for the design, development and self-assessment of effective support services for people with complex needs.

He created the PIElink as a resource for PIEs, was the first editor/curator and wrote much of the pages material, and managed the forums up until 2023, when he began handing over to the new team.

Now trying hard to retire, he lives in Cornwall, where he spends his time writing, gardening and singing, and plays a baritone saxophone with more enthusiasm than skill.